Chris Humphries

D1152528

New Library of Pastoral Care
GENERAL EDITOR: DEREK BLOWS

Love the Stranger

New Library of Pastoral Care
GENERAL EDITOR: DEREK BLOWS

LOVE THE STRANGER

Ministry in Multi-Faith Areas

Roger Hooker
and
Christopher Lamb

First published in Great Britain 1986
SPCK
Holy Trinity Church
Marylebone Road
London NW1 4DU

Acknowledgement:
The extract from the leaflet of the International Society for Krishna
Consciousness is reprinted by permission of the Bhaktivedanta
Book Trust.

British Library Cataloguing in Publication Data

Hooker, Roger
    Love the stranger. — (New Library of pastoral care)
    1. Church work   2. Interdenominational cooperation
    I. Title   II. Lamb, C. A.   III. Series
    259   BV4470

    ISBN 0-281-04244-6

Filmset by Pioneer, Perthshire.
Printed in Great Britain by
the Anchor Press, Tiptree

'If a stranger lives with you in your land, do not molest him. You must count him as one of your own countrymen and love him as yourself.'

Leviticus 19.33

'It is God who sees justice done for the orphan and the widow, who loves the stranger and gives him food and clothing. Love the stranger then, for you were strangers in the land of Egypt.'

Deuteronomy 10.18 − 19

Contents

Foreword

The *New Library of Pastoral Care* has been planned to meet the needs of those people concerned with pastoral care, whether clergy or lay, who seek to improve their knowledge and skills in this field. Equally, it is hoped that it may prove useful to those secular helpers who may wish to understand the role of the pastor.

Pastoral care in every age has drawn from contemporary secular knowledge to inform its understanding of man and his various needs and of the ways in which these needs might be met. Today it is perhaps the secular helping professions of social work, counselling and psychotherapy, and community development which have particular contributions to make to the pastor in his work. Such knowledge does not stand still, and a pastor would have a struggle to keep up with the endless tide of new developments which pour out from these and other disciplines, and to sort out which ideas and practices might be relevant to his particular pastoral needs. Among present-day ideas, for instance, of particular value might be an understanding of the social context of the pastoral task, the dynamics of the helping relationship, the attitudes and skills as well as factual knowledge which might make for effective pastoral intervention, and perhaps most significant of all, the study of particular cases, whether through verbatim reports of interviews or general case presentation. The discovery of ways of learning from what one is doing is becoming increasingly important.

There is always a danger that a pastor who drinks deeply at the well of a secular discipline may lose his grasp of his own pastoral identity and become 'just another' social worker or counsellor. It in no way detracts from the value of these professions to assert that the role and task of the pastor are quite unique among the helping professions and deserve to be clarified and strengthened rather than weakened. The theological commitment of the pastor and the appropriate use of his role will be a recurrent theme of the series. At the same time the pastor cannot afford to work in a vacuum. He needs to be able to communicate and co-operate with those helpers in other disciplines whose work may overlap, without loss of his own unique role. This in turn will mean being able to communicate with them through some understanding of their concepts and language.

Finally, there is a rich variety of styles and approaches in pastoral work within the various religious traditions. No attempt will be made to secure a uniform approach. The Library will contain the variety, and even perhaps occasional eccentricity, which such a title suggests. Some books will be more specifically theological and others more concerned with particular areas of need or practice. It is hoped that all of them will have a usefulness that will reach right across the boundaries of religious denomination.

DEREK BLOWS
Series Editor

Preface

We have written this book for two reasons. The first is that each of us has had the opportunity of serving with churches overseas, Christopher in Pakistan and Roger in India. We were able to learn the main languages of these two countries, Urdu in Pakistan and Hindi in India, and this enabled us to get to know some of the people who live and think in these languages. Our personal friendships meant that we could enter Islam and Hinduism through the minds and hearts of those who live by them, and not simply through books written in English by western scholars. Such books, however reliable and useful they may be, can be seriously misleading if they are not set within the context of personal experience and encounter.

Christopher returned from Pakistan in 1975, but we only met each other for the first time in 1978, when Roger returned from India. We quickly discovered that our pilgrimages, though in important respects very different, had led us independently to some common convictions. We had both found ourselves immeasurably enriched and humbled by the faith of other people. We could not therefore simply dismiss Islam and Hinduism as many (though by no means all) Christians have too easily done in the past. At the same time our discovery of other faiths enhanced and deepened our understanding of our own. This meant that we could not agree with those theologians in Britain who want to relativize all religious commitment, saying that all religions are simply culturally conditioned variations on a single theme. This would make it impossible for Christians or anyone else to have a distinctive message.

Our second reason for writing is that during the last few years our two ministries have been complementary to one another. Since 1979 Christopher has been Co-ordinator of the Other Faiths Theological Project, sponsored jointly by the Bible Churchmen's Missionary Society (BCMS) and the Church Missionary Society (CMS). This has taken him to many parts of Britain, especially to those areas where Asians have settled, in order to discuss with clergy and lay-people the issues raised for Christians by the presence of people of other faiths as fellow-citizens in Britain. Roger's experience has been more local. Since 1982 he has been seconded by CMS to the Diocese of Birmingham for ministry among Asians.

Until comparatively recently the concerns which the two of us so deeply share have been regarded as of only minor significance for other Christians. Now that situation has happily begun to change and to change quite rapidly. Interest in 'other religions' is beginning to show all the signs of becoming a growth industry. Books are now being written, but most of these (some of which we list in Appendix A) are about the theology of religion, and some authors lack the rootedness of personal experience over a long period which we have been able to enjoy. Other books have been written by sociologists who describe different immigrant communities and various aspects of their life. Both types of book are valuable aids to clergy who live and work in multi-faith areas. However, our own meetings and discussions with clergy and others in the last few years have raised a number of questions which the literature which has so far been published ignores. In particular we felt that a book was needed which was addressed, in the first instance, to parochial clergy of the Church of England, showing how they could begin to be involved in ministry among their Asian parishioners, and how they could begin to identify and grapple with the questions which such ministry was bound to raise. Thus our previous experience in Pakistan and India, and our current experience of ministry in this country have converged and produced the conviction that we ought to write this book together.

That background has also determined the kind of book we have tried to write. While it is, we trust, academically respectable we have resisted the temptation to provide an elaborate critical apparatus. In this kind of book too many footnotes can distract the reader's attention, so we have limited them to those which we felt were strictly necessary, and they are grouped together at the end of each chapter. We maintain joint responsibility for what we have written throughout the book, but Chapter 5 records Roger's own experiences, so it appears under his name only, and Appendix D was previously published by Christopher alone, so he is therefore credited as the sole author of it.

We owe much to BCMS and CMS which support Christopher, and to CMS and the Diocese of Birmingham which support Roger. At the same time we are acutely aware of the fact that we could not have written at all without the help of many other people. First among these are the pioneers and scholars of an earlier generation, and in particular we want to single out Max Warren and Kenneth Cragg, who over many years nurtured and encouraged our own involvement and interest in this field. Then, we have both been members of the British Council of Churches' Committee for Relations with People of Other Faiths, or with one or other of its sub-groups, almost since its inception in 1978. This has enabled us to keep in close touch with a wide circle of Christians who share our concerns. As is normal and proper with a BCC committee, this one reflects a wide variety of theological stance and of personal experience. Much of our own thinking has been forged and tested in discussion with these friends. To all of them, and especially to the Committee's tireless secretary, Kenneth Cracknell, we wish to express our gratitude. We would also like to thank the publishers for their guidance and encouragement, and Bishop Lesslie Newbigin, who suggested to them that we should be asked to write the book in the first place.

We owe an incalculable debt to our many friends of other faiths, in Pakistan and India and in Britain. We have frequently been overwhelmed by their hospitality. They have welcomed us into their homes and often into their hearts and lives as well. This book is not simply about them; they are part of all we have written. So too are our wives and children, whose encouragement and criticisms over the months of this book's gestation have been indispensable.

Finally, having recognized this wide network of obligation and support we must dissociate all those to whom we are in

debt from any responsibility for what is written in these
pages. The responsibility for that rests with the two of us
alone.

Christopher Lamb
Roger Hooker
February 1986

ONE

A Ministry to People
Where They Are

'Consider with yourselves the end of your ministry towards the children of God.'

(The Ordering of Priests 1662)

In 1662 it was possible to use a phrase like 'the children of God' and mean without qualification 'the spouse and body of Christ', as the Book of Common Prayer goes on to do. The Anglican priest of those days, as is often noted, was entrusted with the care of a church and congregation which could be assumed without too much self-deception to be conterminous with the whole of local society. His care and ministry was therefore to and within the membership of the Church, as the language of the Ordinal clearly indicates. The occasional person careless or contemptuous of religion was his responsibility as one of 'Christ's sheep that are dispersed abroad', and that phrase was no doubt also intended to cover those who had joined Christian bodies other than the Church of England. What was certainly not intended was a care for those who professed another faith altogether, for in 1662 these amounted only to a tiny handful of Jews who had been readmitted to England by Cromwell after the expulsion of their community by Edward I in 1290. A multi-faith society, as we know it today, would have bewildered and horrified seventeenth-century England, for whom religious faith was the cement of the nation, without which it must fall apart. Religion and loyalty to the established order were inextricably linked, and the only references in the Book of Common Prayer to people of other faiths are that in the notorious Collect for Good Friday which speaks of 'Jews, Turks, Infidels, and Hereticks', and a passage in the Preface introducing the (new) service of Adult Baptism as 'useful for the baptizing of Natives in our Plantations, and others converted to the Faith'.

The Alternative Service Book of 1980 was compiled in a vastly different age. Yet in their anxiety to keep faith and continuity with the Book of 1662 the authors of the Ordinal of 1980 largely failed to reflect the changed circumstances. There is indeed a passing reference to 'a common witness to the world', but the care and ministry of the priest seem again to be focused primarily to and within the membership of the Church: 'The Church and congregation among whom you will serve are one with him (Christ): they are his body. Serve them with joy, build them up in faith, and do all in your power to bring them to loving obedience to Christ.' It may be answered, of course, that the priest's role *is* properly to serve his congregation, and that *with* them he shares in the Church's ministry to the world as a whole. The ministry of the Church, in the sense of its activity rather than its personnel, is not to be equated with the life and witness, however dedicated, of a professional caste within it. Yet the full-time professionals of what is in effect a voluntary society inevitably act as a focus of expectation and understanding of the work of the whole Church, not only for the outsider but also for the insider. If their role is seen primarily as internal to the Church then there is a danger that the whole life of the Church will come to be self-serving, concerned only with the interests of a diminishing band of religious enthusiasts, the rump of a national Church.

Our concern in this book is to resist such a betrayal. Our immediate focus is the Christian responsibility towards people of other faiths living in this country. But in case some glancing through these pages should judge that such a concern is too exotic, too remote from most of Britain, we want to state here our conviction that the issues raised in this responsibility belong with the fundamental assumptions of all Christian ministry. To be in contact as Christians with Hindus, Muslims, Sikhs and Jews is to be reminded that the whole world in all its bewildering human variety is the arena of God's activity, and that, in the Authorized Version's oddly memorable phrase for Acts 10.34, he is no 'respecter of persons'. It is tempting to hide within our churches and become absorbed in their internal affairs. It is tempting too for church authorities to withdraw personnel and money from multi-faith areas on the grounds that the presence of large Muslim, Sikh and Hindu populations automatically diminishes the need for pastoral care. But this is to act on the (usually unstated) premiss that our basic concern is for the maintenance of the existing Christian community, not for its growth or for the welfare of society as a whole. Yet we know that the Church which lives to itself will die by itself.

We hope then that we shall be understood not as protagonists for a particular specialist ministry, but as practitioners of the basic Christian ministry who have been caught up into what is still in Britain the uncommon privilege of close relationships with people who are deeply religious, but outside of the Christian religious tradition. In writing of that particular privilege we intend to write about all Christian ministry.

We shall be concerned primarily with the full-time, ordained Christian minister. Of course, as already acknowledged, Christian ministry does not begin and end with such a person, but it does frequently take its cue from him or her, and he or she generally has both the freedom and the authority to initiate it. We shall take for granted much of the plain good-neighbourliness which many Christians offer (and receive) over the garden wall. This indeed may be Christian ministry, but the word becomes blurred if too freely interpreted. There is a representative character of the person of whom we are thinking which is a significant element in interfaith relations, and which underlines the religious dimension in affairs which might otherwise seem merely secular. Of course there is a grimmer truth involved here too; namely that the blindness or intransigence of a Christian minister can actually prevent the development of this kind of ministry in his congregation. For this reason too we address the ordained minister in particular.

We struggle for clarity with terms like 'Christian ministry'. But there is even greater need for clarity about people of other faiths in Britain, their numbers, character, beliefs and intentions, and the question of Christian responsibilities to them. We are not even sure how many Jews, Muslims, Sikhs, Hindus and Buddhists live in this country, since no official question about religious adherence is ever asked by government record-keepers, and both the communities themselves, and those who feel uneasy about their presence in Britain, are for different reasons inclined to exaggerate their numbers. The absence of official interest in *religious* affiliation (there has of course been considerable controversy about recording *ethnic* identity) is itself an eloquent statement of how religion has become privatized in Britain today compared with the seventeenth century, and is seen as a purely domestic and personal matter of no wider importance. By contrast most countries outside the western world record religious affiliation as a mark of community, and even as an indication of which personal and family law will be applicable in particular cases.

Approximate estimates are as follows: Muslims 800,000 to one million (though Muslims commonly claim 1.5 million); Jews 385,000 (a figure of the Board of Deputies of British Jews); Hindus perhaps 320,000; Sikhs 300,000. The figure for Buddhists is even more difficult to assess, depending on how many of the 100,000 people of Chinese origin resident in Britain would so describe themselves. Jains, Parsees (Zoroastrians) and Baha'is also live in Britain in some thousands, as do the adherents of a multitude of new religious groupings which cannot be dealt with adequately in this book. (We have made some suggestions about Christian attitudes and need for understanding in this area in Appendix C).

More striking than faceless statistics, though not directly pointing to religious affiliation, is the fact that for London as a whole the telephone directory lists more Patels than it does Robinsons, and more Alis than Archers and Atkinses put together, which gives some idea of the likely proportion of Hindus and Muslims among us.

For most people perhaps, culture and religion are an indivisible whole. Very few Greek Cypriots do not belong to the Greek Orthodox Church; very few Turkish Cypriots are anything but Muslims. In Nicosia today the cathedral flies the flag of Greece, while across the Green Line of the divided city the flag of Turkey flutters from the principal mosque. But in other societies religious minorities, of ancient and of modern origin, testify to the significance of religious conviction. White, British-born people have been attracted into all the major world faiths as well as the newer movements. Asian Christians, especially from India and Pakistan, have settled in this country in some thousands, and are often hurt at being thought of as Muslim or Hindu by their white fellow-Christians. Few British people realize that there are more indigenous Christians in India than there are Sikhs, and that the Christians of Kerala in south India look back to St Thomas as their founder. African and Caribbean Christians also add to the splendid diversity of British Christian character.

To many, however, such new and startling variety is difficult to keep pace with. How, for a start, is one to refer to those who are not white and Anglo-Saxon or Celtic? 'Ethnic minorities' has become an accepted term, and it has the merit of including the Italians, Poles, Ukrainians and Greeks who are not usually classed as 'immigrants' despite their recent arrival in Britain. 'Ethnic minorities' is a clumsy term, though, and usually gives way to 'blacks' and 'Asians'. Many Caribbeans have accepted the term 'black' for themselves, even with pride, but its literal meaning in South Asian languages is usually insulting when applied to people. 'Asian' is commonly accepted by people from South Asian countries (India, Pakistan, Bangladesh, Sri Lanka) and by people of Indian descent from East African countries. The Chinese, however, are puzzled at not being regarded as 'Asian', while many Pakistani Muslims see their Muslim identity as more important than their Asian origin, and point out that a Muslim in Britain might be from almost any part of Africa, from the Middle East, Pakistan, Bangladesh, Malaysia or even an Eastern European country like Yugoslavia. And 'Paki', after all has joined 'nigger' as a term of abuse. We settle for 'Asian' as being the least problematic.

But the demographic confusion is nothing to the theological. A white worshipper coming out of her church met an Indian Christian lady on her way in for the service in Punjabi and decided to make contact: 'Have you come to worship your prophet Muhammad?' she tried, thereby dropping a record number of bricks. Another favourite is the Scottish lady who ended a diatribe against the Ayatollah Khomeini with the damning indictment: ' . . . and he calls himself a *Christian!'*

For it is a new and strange thing to many to appreciate that
Christianity is no longer the only practical religious option in
Britain; that now 'religious' does not necessarily mean
'Christian'. It will take people some time to catch up. The
normal assumption of many British people with a certain
affection for the Church, but very little understanding of
what its inner life is like, is that one religion is much the same
as another and quite as good. It is important to remember
that this conviction exists side by side, often in the same
head, with the equally firm conviction that Muslims are
fatalistic polygamists with a tendency to fanaticism and
violence, while God is a rather gullible old man who speaks
seventeenth-century English and cannot understand computers.
For few of us are logical. Sometimes that can be an advantage,
but in the English (if not the Scots, Welsh and Irish) case the
condition is combined with a distrust of intellectuals in
general and theologians in particular.

The result is a desperate need for clarity, particularly
about the aims of the Church in a multi-faith society. What is
the relationship of Christianity to other faiths, and what does
this imply for the life and ministry of the Church? Here are
theological questions with profound practical implications.
Even if, in typically English fashion, we attempt to ignore the
theological issues and 'simply be practical' the religious
character of the people we are dealing with makes that course
impossible. So some social workers brought up with an
indifference to religion find themselves up against Muslim
convictions about dietary law or modest dress or the kind of
marriage permitted to Muslims, and are compelled to
acknowledge that such people are religiously, not just
racially and culturally, distinct. Similarly a Christian lady,
invited to entertain a Sikh lady to tea as part of One World
Week, asks uneasily: 'What is the aim of this? Are we trying
to Christianize them?' To answer with an unqualified 'Of
course!' is likely to produce an extremely tense and unnatural
meeting, if not a very angry Sikh lady. To disavow evangelism
altogether, on the other hand, is to make nonsense of centuries
of Christian witness and to dishonour Christ himself by the
implication that he is only for the Christian. We write of
some of these issues in more detail later.

As soon as we speak of centuries of Christian witness,

however, we are compelled to recognize that, as one distinguished Sri Lankan bishop put it, we have been 'nurtured in the context of imperialism and Christian triumphalism'.[1] Even within the British Isles the English have alleged Scottish meanness, Irish stupidity, and Welsh dishonesty ('Taffy was a Welshman, Taffy was a thief . . .'). The charges may be light-hearted today, but the dictionary confirms that 'Welsh', like 'Jew' and 'Turk', has been given a disreputable meaning in our language.[2] Such nationalist sentiment is found, of course, all over the world, but for a people who ruled over many millions of others it served a special purpose. If the Celt or the 'native' is unintelligent or unreliable we can feel justified in making decisions for them. In the same way, we need not take their religion seriously.

It is easy to be wiser than our fathers, and adventurers like Cecil Rhodes left plenty of hostages to fortune in the shape of speeches we now blush to read. The missionary movement of the nineteenth (and earlier) centuries was inevitably intertwined with commercial and other motives and it is not difficult, though seriously mistaken, to read it as essentially a by-product of western expansion, part of its ideological underpinning, now properly discarded.

Some writers point to the 'failure' of the missionary movement to make any significant impact on most of Asia in numerical terms, and conclude that the missionary motive is as obsolete as the sola topi. The truth of history is very much more complicated. When the East India Company dismissed a chaplain for distributing tracts to Indians Warren Hastings remarked that 'the man who could be rash enough to speak of Christ to the natives would let off a pistol in a powder magazine'. Similar instances of clashes between missionary and colonial administrator abound. Nor should the Christian impact on Asia be reckoned only in terms of numbers, though the presence of Christian churches in every Asian country is a testimony to much missionary heroism. Curiously the revival of other faiths has been in no small measure due to the Christian challenge to deeply conservative societies. 'Missionary dedication' and 'missionary zeal' are phrases which constantly appear in Pakistani or Indian newspapers today as politicians search for images to spur their people to good works in the development of the nation. The fact is that

missionary history has never been taken seriously either by
church or secular historians in Britain, and the result is the
caricature of missionary personnel which features in books
like Paul Scott's *Raj Quartet,* in the pathetic Barbie.

But history holds deeper problems for the Christian than
these issues from the age of imperialism. Judaism and Islam
in particular, and other faiths in general have been the subject
of sustained defamation by Christian theologians over many
centuries. James Parkes was one of the first Christians to
document this in the case of Judaism in the 1930s, and
Norman Daniel has since done a similar service for Islam.[3]
Why should it have been necessary to distort the beliefs of
others and drag their reputation through the mud in order to
preach Christ? Was Christian faith so weak, so inherently
fragile, that its exponents had to resort to such tactics? The
answer of course parallels the case of missionary and colonial
interpenetration. Motives were mixed, and people assumed
that victory had to be achieved by whatever means. One of
the results, however, is that many people have become
suspicious of missionary propaganda, and in the present
climate of pessimism about western culture, have come to the
conclusion that religious traditions other than the Christian
are of equal validity, at least for those nourished from birth
within them.

These wider considerations reinforce the perception of
many sensitive consciences that Britain is a deeply racist
society. To the outrage of tests for virginity conducted at
Heathrow Airport on brides-to-be arriving from South Asia
we have added racial harassment to the point of murder, a
profoundly unjust Nationality Act, continuing discrimination
in employment and a multitude of minor offences like the
daubing of offensive slogans on synagogues, mosques,
temples and even Jewish and Muslim cemeteries. It is difficult
to appreciate the cumulative effect of such hostility on people's
lives, and the deep sense of vulnerability which results.
Paranoia is understandable. As the Jew said: 'Just because
you're paranoid, it doesn't mean they're not out to get you!' In
an environment perceived as alien if not actively hostile
people naturally take refuge in their own ethnic community,
and renew their loyalty to its focus, which is often the place of
worship. In fact for most South Asians, the mosque, temple

or gurdwara (for Sikhs) is the only place of meeting outside the home where they can be themselves.

What can be the character of Christian ministry, and more important, what will be its motive, in such a situation? Does evangelism have any place at all? And if service alone is thought appropriate because explicit speaking for Christ is thought offensive or aggressive, what will be the underlying motive of that service? Is it to be some Christian reparation for past Christian-inflicted ills? So people have often advocated in the case of the Jews. Yet we may wonder if service with such a guilty conscience can ever create a healthy relationship between the server and the served. Then what is wrong with simple response to need as a motive for ministry? Nothing, except that people are not always in need, and at all times resist definition of themselves solely in terms of need. They are people created for relationships with other people, and only the offer of such relationship can begin to acknowledge the fullness of their humanity. But relationship must be between equals who work towards complete openness with one another. It follows that there can be no determination at the outset to speak of everything *except* our faith, no will to exclude the *possibility* that the person of another faith might accept the Christian faith because of us, and no pretence of *indifference* as to whether that might happen or not. We all have to run the risk of being changed.

We would contend the Christian ministry in its true character is implicitly evangelistic. Ultimate questions about the nature and being of God are always implicit in the faithful offer of Christian love and service, whether they are openly stated or not. Of course service has its own integrity, and cannot be faithfully offered as a bribe or an inducement towards conversion. People may assume that the motive is guilt, or the need for reparation, or even a destiny which compels such expiation for past sin, but Christians will often see gratitude as the most compelling reason for what they do, thanksgiving for God made known in Christ. Such gratitude is always likely to find expression in word as well as in deed.

We believe that the widespread unease about evangelism, both outside and inside the Church, has arisen because we have allowed it to become separate from the whole life and work of the Church, so that it is something done by special people in special ways. That particular ministry is necessary, yet the evangelical message should be implicit in the whole. The lady who was to be hostess at the One World Week tea-party could simply have got on with the offering of hospitality to a Sikh lady in the confidence that the genuine offering of care and concern to someone of another culture and religion is itself evangelistic, though not of course the whole of evangelism. It is good news that someone cares, and when that caring cannot be separated from a Christian conviction and loyalty there is already an unspoken Christian message. It is the articulation of that message that requires a delicacy of touch and a spiritual sensitivity.

There is no doubt, however, that such sensitivity has often been lacking, and many British Christians have felt that the forms of evangelism they were familiar with could only be seen as a kind of aggression when used with other faith communities who already felt themselves deeply threatened in British society. Others found themselves genuinely moved by the dedication and depth of disciplined devotion of new friends of another faith, and frankly adjusted their theology to fit these new discoveries. John Hick is among the most distinguished to have made such a 'spiritual pilgrimage'.

> Occasionally attending worship in mosque and synagogue, temple and gurdwara, it was evident that essentially the same kind of thing is taking place in them as in a Christian church — namely, human beings opening their minds to a higher divine Reality, known as personal and good and as demanding righteousness and love between man and man. I could see that . . . each faith is, naturally enough, perceived by its adherents as being unique and absolute.[4]

Again it is vital to recognize that the common ground between faiths is real and authentic, if limited, and that particular individuals from different faith communities may discover in each other a remarkable convergence of spiritual understanding, the more appreciated because it was so unexpected. An experienced clergyman who is in no way a follower of John Hick has written to one of us about the development of 'a very deep bond of friendship with our local Rabbi . . . I have found my attitude to Jewish people changing quite radically and a friendship growing which seems to me to be the witness of the Holy Spirit.'

Some find themselves disconcerted, not only by the theology of John Hick, but by the continual concessions they feel people are urging them to make to the validity and authenticity of other faiths. The substantive issue of the status of other faiths in Christian eyes is taken up in our last chapter, and here it must suffice to say that we do not accept the viewpoint of John Hick. But the demand to concede advantages in general is no new one. Indeed the great CMS missionary to Muslims, Temple Gairdner (1873–1928), wrote of Islam in a style which deliberately emphasized the power and significance of that faith. *The Reproach of Islam* (1909) poses the question in the rhetorical style of the day:

> Why must we for ever renounce all the favourable conditions, giving, like the Scottish King at Flodden, *all* the advantages to the opponent? Why must we strive always up the hill, the wind and the rain for ever driving in our faces; ever, ever conceding, never, never receiving the handicap and the odds! . . . If Islam's forces are indeed nature, the world and the flesh, then Islam has left us one weapon in taking away all the others—it has abandoned to us the Sword of *the Spirit—the Spirit of Jesus is the only asset of the Church.*[5]

There are of course immense differences between Cairo in the first decades of this century and Britain in the 1980s, yet Gairdner's principle is surely right. Unless we concede all the points above, and others too, and make them more cogently than space allows here, our ministry to those of other faiths will always be in danger of actually being (not simply seeming) a kind of exploitation, a new religious imperialism, a theological form of racial harassment. If it be objected that this is asking too much we have to answer with Kenneth Cragg that 'mission is not a calculus of success, but an obligation in love . . . We present Christ for the sole, sufficient reason that He deserves to be presented.' Mission and ministry in true Christian intention are not attempts to manipulate other people. They are an obligation in love which leaves no room for any sense of superiority or the arrogance of which those who speak of mission to those of other faiths are sometimes accused. We have continually to recall that the costly truth of the gospel we live for and try to live out has to be matched by an equal costliness and integrity in the manner of our discipleship. The first part of that cost is the recognition that the history of Christian relations with those of other faiths is for the most part a very dismal tale, and that we inevitably carry the burden of that history with us into every new relationship.

Missionaries have to learn this lesson very quickly, and come to terms through their own inner resources with the fact that some people will always associate a white face with the injustices of the past and the continuing inequalities of the present. If we can learn to bear the burden of sinfulness in this way while working to undo its effects we shall come to demonstrate the meaning of redemption in our own lives. The well-known definition of the Sri Lankan theologian D. T. Niles is permanently relevant: 'Evangelism is one beggar telling another beggar where to find bread.' A whole-hearted acceptance of the spiritual bankruptcy and beggarliness of our culture wherever it has departed from the ways and words of Christ will remove the taint of the 'arrogance' many associate with the work of the Church in relation to those of other faiths.

We bear the burden of our collective past. We bear the burden of present misunderstanding — not only from those of other faiths but often also from fellow-Christians and colleagues. But we are sustained by the learning which goes on within that fundamental obligation of love. As we hope to show in what follows, there is immense richness in this ministry. As for motive, we are content to say with Paul: 'It is not ourselves that we proclaim; we proclaim Christ Jesus as Lord, and ourselves as your servants, for Jesus' sake' (2 Cor. 4.5).

Notes

1. Wickremesinghe, L., *Togetherness and Uniqueness — Living Faiths in Inter-Relation.* The Second Lambeth Interfaith Lecture (13 June 1979), p.10.

2. In 1973 an action was brought against the Clarendon Press claiming that the secondary definitions of the word 'Jew' were 'derogatory, defamatory and deplorable', and asking for an injunction to be placed on any Oxford dictionary that included them. The Press claimed that the inclusion of such meanings did not bestow on them any significance beyond what they possessed already, and the action failed. (*The Times,* 25 June 1981)
3. Parkes, J., *The Conflict of the Church and the Synagogue. A Study in the Origins of Anti-Semitism.* London 1935. Daniel, N., *Islam and the West. The Making of an Image.* Edinburgh University Press 1960.
4. Hick, J., *God has Many Names* (Macmillan 1980), p. 5.
5. Quoted in Padwick, C., *Temple Gairdner of Cairo* (London, SPCK 1929), p. 184 f.

TWO

Starting Points

———

Let us suppose that a vicar ministers in a parish where Asians also live, and that he accepts the argument of the previous chapter. Where does he start? How does he begin to make contact? Apart from an occasional 'good morning' and a smile to those he passes in the street, he has no natural way of meeting the Asians, who for the most part are well content with this state of affairs. Their communities seem somewhat enclosed and they display no obvious desire to meet him or his flock.

Let us assume, then, as a minimum, that the minister feels he ought to establish relations of good neighbourliness and Christian love with the Asians who live in his parish. This means he has deliberately to set about meeting them. Let us also assume, for the moment, that he is acting on an individual basis. To the large and important question of how his congregation can and should be involved in the enterprise we shall turn in chapter 3. Also, since this is a book written by Anglicans primarily for other Anglicans we leave out the ecumenical dimension, not because it is unimportant, but because it would make the argument of the book unnecessarily complicated. We hope that much of what we write may be of use to Christians of other denominations, but they too will have their own distinctive approach to the subject.

There is another and more positive reason for beginning with the minister as a Christian individual. The initial approaches to members of another community are best undertaken on an informal and casual basis. They cannot remain on this level, but this is the most appropriate way for them to start.

One way of meeting strangers is to 'loiter with intent' in the places where they are most likely to be found. To loiter, according to the Shorter Oxford English Dictionary, means 'to linger indolently on one's way; to hang idly about a place; to dawdle over a task. To travel indolently and with frequent pauses.' It is interesting that the word was 'perhaps introduced (into English) by vagrants from the Low Countries.' The minister can deliberately set aside time, say one or two afternoons a month, to loiter in a particular area. He can drop in on shops. Shopkeepers, Asian or other, are always willing to talk to strangers, for that is part of their job. This means that they have fewer inhibitions than many other people, but one needs to find out when are the slack periods when they have time to talk. While one is talking other customers are likely to drop in too. Sometimes they are willing to talk in a way they would be reluctant to do in the street, for a shop provides a defined and circumscribed context in which people can feel more secure than they do outside.

But it is also possible to talk to people in the street, especially if one is walking in the same direction, and here too, one needs to discover the main routes by which people walk to shopping centres and other places such as the local school, and the times of day when they can be met there.

What about visiting places of worship? Certainly visitors are usually made to feel welcome in temples, gurdwaras and mosques. Unlike most churches they are nearly always open and someone is there, for these places are often the focal point for the social life of the community concerned. If one goes in, one does so as a guest and so it is important to observe the courtesies—taking off one's shoes for example. To be a guest is also to be in a position of comparative weakness compared with one's host, for he is on his home ground. This is no bad foundation for meeting.

Yet some Christians are reluctant to enter the place of worship belonging to another faith. This may be nothing more than natural shyness and fear of the unknown, but it may have deeper and more theological roots. They feel that to enter another place of worship is to condone what goes on inside it, and this they are not prepared to do. Whether we go in or not it is important to think through the reasons for our decision. It is also a salutary exercise to try to justify our views to those who take the opposite course.

In the early stages of his loitering, perhaps for six months or a year, the minister may think nothing is happening. His contacts are few and fragile, he may meet with indifference or suspicion, he feels as if he is getting nowhere and is just wasting his time. In fact a great deal is happening. People are sizing him up, wondering what his motives are, perhaps asking themselves or each other if he can really be trusted. This is true in the early stages of any ministry. For example, a nurse once agreed to run a church youth club, something she had never done before. She proved to be very good at it but later commented: 'For the first six months I just hung about on the edges wondering what on earth I was supposed to be doing.' Every minister has to live through this period of apparent uselessness, resisting the temptation to justify his activity in some other way. He may want to set up some sort of organization, but this is unwise for it will not be rooted in the felt needs of the local community, nor will it have their confidence. It may take up a lot of his time but it will prevent him from actually meeting people. There is no substitute for waiting and for patience. One form of unbelief is to attempt something before its proper time.

Because this preliminary stage is so important we must look at it more closely. Chatting to people on the streets and in shops may seem to be a trivial activity and often that is just what it is. It is integrity of purpose and the discipline of waiting which can redeem it from triviality. Many, perhaps all, personal relationships begin on this level, but their worth is to be judged not by where they begin but by how they continue and where they lead.

A Christian who has pondered on the meaning of the walk to Emmaus will not lightly dismiss talking to strangers on the street as a waste of time, nor will he be much impressed by those who say that this is an unwarrantable intrusion into other people's lives. For to refuse to talk to the people one passes is in principle to pass by on the other side — even and indeed especially if one is actually walking on the same side of the street.

All Christian ministry is, to begin with, a kind of interference, but then so too was the ministry of Christ. The minister needs to be sensitive to the dangers of trying to manipulate people. He will recall that the Christ of the

Emmaus Road 'made as if he would go further', and it was only when he was actually invited in that he joined the two disciples for a meal. His hesitation can no doubt be interpreted in different ways but at the very least it points to the fact that he will not barge his way into people's lives: nor may we.

Another incident in the Gospels enables us to come at the same point from another angle: when Jesus washes the disciples' feet he has to kneel, to speak to them he has to look up into their faces. He cannot look down on them. That can provide a valuable yard-stick by which to assess all our relationships. The cancer of racism is present in us all. One form it can take is an unconsciously patronizing attitude towards people who are different. Most of us are unaware of what our attitudes truly are for they are rooted in our unconscious minds, yet they are conveyed by our gestures and by the look in our eye. Those to whom we speak are often more aware of what is really in our hearts than we are ourselves. People from another culture who become genuine friends can often alert us to these things.

But we must return to our loitering. It depends on a distinctively Christian attitude to people. It also depends on a distinctive understanding of both time and work, for outwardly there is nothing to distinguish it from mere laziness. 'Is it your day off today?' is a question the loiterer may find himself having to answer. To loiter effectively he needs to be relaxed, and this is impossible if he is feeling guilty about wasting his time.

Yet most of us have the opposite problem, indeed, any minister who has persisted in reading this book so far will be tempted at this point to throw it aside in irritation. 'This is totally unrealistic,' he will say, 'How can I possibly make time in my own ministry for what is being advocated here?'

Let us frankly acknowledge that most clergy today are under greater pressure than they were even ten or fifteen years ago. Running the church, or encouraging and enabling lay people to run it, the normal and continual demands of pastoral care and visiting, helping lay people—and being helped themselves *by* lay people—to discover and appropriate the faith more deeply, such activities consume all, and sometimes, it can seem, more than all his time and energy.

On top of this he may well feel that many of the old

securities on which he used to depend have vanished. The central doctrines of the faith are now questioned, and questioned openly: how can the hard-pressed minister find the time, let alone provide himself with the equipment to grapple with these issues for himself?

He has to live, like many other people, in a constant tension between the urgent and the important: the urgent clamours for his immediate attention. A bereaved family must be visited before the funeral, a sermon has to be prepared, papers must be read and mastered for an important diocesan meeting, letters must be answered. The pressure can seem relentless and unending.

By contrast the important can always be postponed indefinitely: the new book there is no time to read—even supposing there is money to buy it—the family with no church connection whom one promised to visit at some unspecified date, the quiet day or retreat which one always intends but somehow never actually has.

The minister needs a measure of self-awareness as he faces this tension within his own life. The person who submits to the tyranny of the urgent can gradually and unknowingly become incapable of living in any other way. Just as someone who has been unemployed for a long time can become almost incapable of living once again within the disciplines which a job demands (in the unlikely event of one becoming available), so too the person whose days consist in a ceaseless dash from one thing to the next can become almost incapable of living according to a different rhythm.

This is not all, for even if the minister does manage to allot a modest portion of his time to ministry among the local Asians, he will find himself subject to the pressures of a subtle and usually unrecognized dynamic which pull him away from this frontier and back into the routine life of the Church.

This dynamic seems to be universal and does not only apply to hard-pressed parochial clergy in England. Again and again Christians who are on the frontiers seem to be drawn away from spending their time with those who do not share their faith, to spending it—for entirely good and honourable reasons—among those who do.

In 1958 Bishop John V. Taylor wrote a book called *The*

Growth of the Church in Buganda. In it he used the phrase 'the withdrawal of the missionary upwards and sideways.' When the missionaries arrived in a place where the Church did not exist they had to spend all their time talking with people who were not Christians. There was after all, no-one else to talk to and nothing else to do. But when some of the local people responded to the gospel and asked for baptism that situation changed: now the missionaries began to find their time increasingly taken up with the teaching and pastoral care of the new converts, and with running the affairs of the growing church. The 'withdrawal' to which Bishop Taylor refers was sideways into administration and upwards into control.

The implications of that withdrawal were and are enormous, but in this book we are concerned with only one of them: gradually regular face-to-face contact with those who were not Christians was lost.[1]

Something very similar happened in North India, though in a different way and for different reasons. This is the heartland of Hinduism, where responses to the gospel in terms of baptism have been very few indeed — the opposite situation to the one Bishop Taylor describes. But this is an area which abounds in great Christian institutions — schools, colleges, hospitals, a famous and pioneering agricultural centre. These places have certainly made a profound impact upon Hindus over a long period. They have also provided a context for the loyal and devoted service of many Christian workers. Yet at the same time they have taken Christians away from face-to-face meeting with Hindus and others. Of course such meetings have taken place, but they have been on Christian territory, and therefore on Christian terms. Donald McGavran once argued that the building of these institutions was an unconscious substitute for the Church's failure in evangelism. So here too there was a withdrawal from the frontiers.

Nearer home and more recently the same process is evident: during the first year or two of their ministry industrial chaplains find that they can devote much of their time to meeting people on the shop floor, but gradually they find themselves pulled away into other things which in themselves are excellent and unexceptionable, but which involve them more and more with other Christians. We all find that regular and secure activities reinforce our need to be useful and to succeed.

So too, Kenneth Cracknell, Secretary of the British Council of Churches' Committee for Relations with People of Other Faiths wrote in 1981:

> During the last three years of travelling throughout England, Scotland and Wales I have learnt that it is normally of no value to ask church leaders, parish priests, secretaries of Christian Councils and the like about the extent of interfaith activity taking place in their area. For such people pastoral concerns (the shepherding of the flock with all the manifold implications of this) leave little time for their personal involvement on the very frontiers of the churches' life in the world. Those out front are often impatient in turn with those maintaining the bases and don't send communiqués back, and yet in the name of Christ they are engaged in new and pioneering enterprises. So the question is always: how does one find these pioneering people?

Is it therefore realistic to expect an already hard-pressed parish priest to become such a pioneering person, even if only in a modest amount of his time? And even if it is realistic, how can he resist that dynamic which will always draw him away from such a role? What we are talking about, then, is not merely the question of finding time in which to loiter, but the question of finding the inner resources which can sustain one in a way of spending time which can yield no immediate or obvious results. It is perhaps the difficulty of doing that which prevents many people from ever starting in the first place, and which makes so many of those who do start surrender to the dynamic which we have just described.

Part of the solution to this difficulty is to be found, paradoxically, in the life of the very Asian community which the minister longs to reach. Many of its members will have been brought up in the villages of the Indian sub-continent, where life is lived according to the rhythms of nature, and where time is still not measured by the hands of a clock and so does not have to be filled. Even those whose formative years were spent in the cities are still psychologically closer to the patterns of village life than we are in the West.

Consequently in this country as in Asia, hospitality still tends to be spontaneous rather than elaborately planned in advance, and it is the height of ill manners to look at one's watch and say: 'I have to go now, I have another engagement.'

Part of the difficulty of ministering among Asians is therefore that more often than not it means almost literally stepping into another world, not simply moving on to another engagement in the same one. This makes searching psychological and spiritual demands on the minister, for he is now in a very real sense no longer at home. Yet it is precisely these demands which are a potential source of enrichment: as one submits to the costly discipline of moving from one world to the other and back again the transition does become imperceptibly easier. In time one can come positively to relish slipping into the Asian rhythm which can then become a resource for one's own living. In its light our preoccupation with the urgent can be revealed as a superficial form of escapism, which like most kinds of escapism is also a prison.

The great writers on prayer will often tell us that God is most truly present in those very experiences which seem to deny him. It is this which lies at the heart of the walk to Emmaus, to which we have already referred. There is much in these same writers about the consecration of time, for example de Caussade's *On Self-Abandonment to Divine Providence* speaks of the sacrament of the present moment: at every moment God provides us with something to do or to suffer. Our business is with obedience to him at that moment, not with what comes before or after. Time seen in this way can become an occasion for recognizing opportunities, instead of a mad rush of endless activity.

It is this inward consecration of time which alters its significance and so enables the minister deliberately to *make* time for loitering.

What of the loiterer's attitude to work? Apparently he is not doing any, which is why the very word has pejorative overtones. To loiter is to be suspected of being up to no good. What does the Christian loiterer expect to achieve? What results can he show, and how can he justify this use of time to others?

In fact his whole attitude contains an implicit challenge to the conventional wisdom which says we must set ourselves

objectives and measure our success or failure in achieving
them. The loiterer so to speak hands over his objectives to
those whom he is trying to reach, so that success or failure
are now in their hands and not in his.

What he wants and prays for is, in the first instance,
response — a response to his own presence. The response
may take the form of a friendly smile of recognition, questions
about himself, whether asked from idle curiosity or genuine
interest, or an invitation to come into someone's home. A
response is the gift by one person of part of himself to
another, and this means it can never be compelled or
commanded but only evoked. One has to wait for it to be
freely given, and if it is, treat it with the utmost reverence. It
will probably be given at a time and in a manner that one
least expects. It may never be given at all.

Loitering is therefore a peculiarly vulnerable activity. It
cannot be justified in terms of results, least of all to those
whose working life can and must be so justified. The teacher,
the social worker, the doctor or nurse, the business man or
the civil servant all have to answer in terms of results for the
way they spend their time. So many children have passed
exams, so many clients or patients have been seen, so much
profit has been made. Yet all know that the more precisely
their results are assessed the more elusive becomes the true
significance of what they are doing, for they are all dealing
with people, and unless the human relationships of their
enterprise are right the results will not come out right either.
Indeed there must always be a tension between the results at
which they aim and the relationships which are necessary to
achieve them, for relationships can never finally be made to
serve an end beyond themselves.

The distinctive mark of our loiterer is that his sole aim is to
establish relationships with other people. Where these
relationships will finally lead him and them is unpredictable,
for it all depends on the Holy Spirit. But at this stage we are
concerned not with ends but with beginnings. All
relationships have to begin with talking to another person.
What does one talk about? The late Bishop Ian Ramsey had
the great gift of getting alongside people very quickly and
someone once asked him how he did so. He replied: 'When I

meet someone for the first time I look for their enthusiasms, for enthusiasm is not very far from worship.'

Most people enjoy being 'drawn out' and talking about themselves, and Asians are no exception to this. They will happily talk of their families, their personal story, of what they think of Britain and the British. The possible topics of conversation are endless, but what one cannot do is work out in advance a shared agenda or set of objectives, as abstract theories of 'dialogue' can sometimes suggest. The important thing is not to make plans but to relax, and to be willing to move when and where the Spirit leads.

It is also worth remembering that the trust and confidence for which we long are gifts which other people are entitled to give or to withold. They will be the more willing and ready to offer this gift if we are willing to talk about ourselves and our concerns, and so make a gift of ourselves first.

One hazard in making conversation across cultural, in this case Asian boundaries, is that it may mean something subtly different to the two parties concerned. Asians from village backgrounds may appear to be interested in only a limited range of subjects, and in that case part of our ministry may be to try to enlarge their awareness. Sometimes too there may be great tracts of silence, and this tends to be more acceptable and so natural in Asian social intercourse than our own. Or again, the minister may find himself ignored while his hosts talk among themselves. This is not discourtesy, it is simply part of the way in which Asian societies work. In the same way it is perfectly acceptable to pick up a newspaper or a magazine in the presence of a guest and start to read it, while in our own culture that is normally very rude. Language can also be a barrier, but there are many Asians who can speak English.

But let us now suppose that the loiterer is on terms of more than nodding aquaintance with a number of people, some of whom he will be able to visit in their homes. What does he do next? The answer is, if he is wise, nothing at all. Others will ask him to do things for them. Such requests are likely to be of two kinds, both of them related to the way in which Asians perceive him. As a white religious leader he is presumed to have influence. He may be asked to help in trying to get a relation admitted to this country, or to track down a daughter who has run away from home. His equivalent in the societies of the Indian sub-continent would normally have such influence and be expected to use it, but the English clergyman finds such expectations embarrassing, for he knows he cannot fulfil them. Yet as a minimum he will probably want to do what he can to help in such cases, and this may mean putting the person concerned in touch with the appropriate advisers. At the same time, to try to explain why the help he himself can offer is limited can be one way of educating his new friends in the nature of British society.

The second kind of request relates more directly to his religious role. He may be asked to say prayers at a Sikh funeral in order to prevent the spirit of the dead person from troubling the surviving relations. One of us was asked to supply a picture of Jesus to be placed alongside the pictures of the Sikh gurus, to say prayers in the home of a recently bereaved family, and to bless a garage.

These are all genuine examples of what has actually happened. They are all requests which may make the minister feel deeply uneasy. Should a Christian minister say prayers at or even after a Sikh funeral? Should he be blessing a home for someone of another religion? Would not the gift of a picture of Jesus be an endorsement of syncretism? To say 'Yes' looks like a betrayal of his faith, yet to say 'No' could cause hurt and misunderstanding. Even if he does decide to do what is asked of him he may find himself looking nervously over his shoulder at his congregation, wondering what they would think if they knew what he was up to. He would do much better to tell them straightaway and indeed to ask for their help in working out the issues involved. If he does not tell them he will very quickly find himself leading a double life—but this is to anticipate chapter 4.

His immediate task is not to say either yes or no to what is asked of him, but to try to understand the meaning of the request. The people of the other religion speak from a set of assumptions and presuppositions which are different from his own. The more he has studied the other religion the more easily he will understand what is said to him. But not everyone can become an authority on other religions. The minister needs to know when he is out of his depth, and to know where he can find the help he needs.

Before looking at these requests in more detail it is worth pondering what happens in any conversation. The world of music affords a useful analogy for this: when I am listening to a great concerto my mind is focused on the solo instrument, but its edges, of which I am only half aware, are attuned to the orchestral background. In a conversation the amount of shared 'orchestral background' will vary. With my close friends it will be very large. As we say, 'We have a lot in common.' We can say almost anything we like to one another, in the confidence that we will be understood. It is this confidence which makes humour possible, for it always appeals to a set of shared assumptions which are not articulated. It depends on what is left unsaid, and a joke which has to be explained has ceased to be a joke. Shared laughter is a sign of intimacy. The negative corollary of this is that 'foreigners have no sense of humour.' The reason why this is true is that humour is normally specific to particular cultures. To be the foreigner and not to know what the locals are laughing at can be a very lonely experience. For that reason it is unwise to risk humour across cultural frontiers until one knows people very well indeed.

With the kind of requests we are considering the people who make them are, like the rest of us, at home within their own language and culture. They assume, without actually thinking about it, that the Christian minister to whom they are talking lives in the same mental world and shares the same background assumptions. Part of his proper professional skill is to be able to recognize when this is not the case. When he can do this he can not only listen to what they actually say, but also be attuned to what they are unconsciously speaking from, their asumptions and pre-suppositions, which he must learn to distinguish from his own.

In the light of these insights let us now examine the particular requests which we have already listed. Why should a Christian minister be asked to say prayers at a Sikh funeral? In this case he first went to the house to find out exactly what was wanted and why. He discovered that a young man had been killed in a road accident. His brother said to the minister: 'I don't know what you people do, but we bang nails into the door-posts and say prayers as the coffin is taken out of the house.' 'But why don't you ask your own man to do this—I am a Christian?' 'He is not here, and we have a family wedding in two weeks. We want to make sure there isn't any trouble.'

The background to these words is roughly as follows: this man died before his time. Such deaths are always due to sickness, violence or, as here, to accident, and the ghost of the dead person, being dissatisfied, will return to haunt the surviving relations unless they take specific steps to prevent it. Metal is a standard protection against such evil spirits, and the threshold, being the place of access to the house, is particularly vulnerable to attack. The prayers of an appropriate ritual specialist are a useful if not a necessary addition.

This is not Sikhism but a piece of folk religion which has parallels in many other cultures including our own. Do we not still use horse-shoes as door-knockers, or hang them over our lintels? If he remembers this the minister may well hesitate before dismissing this request as 'mere superstition'. (His hesitancy will be further strengthened if he has read a little anthropology.) He may also find himself reflecting on the nature of grief. We do not, in our society, talk of being haunted by the ghosts of dead relations, but we certainly know the experience to which those words point. Our lives can be 'haunted' if not crippled by the memories of past hurts inflicted by those long dead—or by ourselves upon them, or by the manner and time of their dying. We internalize grief and have given up the rituals which set the boundaries for its expression, so instead of wearing black arm-bands we need 'bereavement counsellors'.

Such reflections as these may well make the minister feel that the original request is much less strange than he thought it was when it was first made. In this case he did go to the house and said prayers at the threshold in the presence of a few of the relatives who had stayed behind after the funeral party had left. He prayed not 'through Jesus Christ our Lord' but 'in the name of the Lord Jesus Christ'. While the former phrase incorporates all who are present in the intention of the prayer, making the assumption that they are Christians, the latter does not and so betrays no-one's integrity. These distinctions are more important for the person who says the prayer and for the occasion itself rather than for the family. For them the words convey not meaning but power, in this case the power of protection from a ghost.

However, the minister felt that to say this prayer and then to do no more would indeed be to compromise himself and his faith. After a few weeks he went back to the house where he was greeted with surprise: 'What's the matter? Didn't you get paid?' He replied that he had neither been paid nor wanted to be, but had come to offer sympathy to the family in their loss, and to see how they were getting on. He also gave them a copy of St Luke's Gospel in Punjabi, suggesting that they read it since 'It was in the name of the Lord whose story is told in this book that I prayed on that day.' Whether the family actually read it is doubtful, but at least the possibility was there. The minister now visits the family regularly and has a warm relationship with them. Where that may lead him and them no-one can tell, for the story is not yet over.

What of the request to bless a garage? This too is not so incongruous as it might appear at first sight. The owner's previous garage-repair shop had been burnt down. He was anxious for the safety of the new one since his livelihood depended on it. The desire for blessing and prosperity is universal; the Psalms are full of prayers for it, and why do Anglicans keep Rogation Sunday? Of course an Anglo-Saxon garage owner is unlikely to ask the local vicar to come and bless it, but this Sikh was a much less secularized man, who still believed in the power of sacred words.

The request to supply a picture of Jesus was also concerned with power. The family were in considerable distress since father was unemployed and mother suffered from severe depression. Many Asian homes have cheap coloured pictures on the walls of the sitting-room. These indicate the religious allegiance of those who live in the house. They may be of the Sikh gurus or of some of the Hindu gods. Muslim homes will often have pictures of Mecca. Asian Christians will display pictures of Jesus. Often these are of the Sacred Heart, for popular art of this kind is very much part of the Catholic tradition, while it is found much less among Protestants.

The request for such a picture of Jesus was at least a recognition that here was a source of power which might help the family. So here too, when the minister gave the family the picture he also gave them a Gospel, suggesting that they should read about the one for whose picture they had asked.

This incident too, is part of a continual relationship of 'dropping in' and pastoral concern.

The request to say prayers at a Hindu home after a relative had died in India was rather different, for the significance only emerged later. The minister went to the house, with his wife who had also been invited, and used some of the prayers from the ASB funeral service, again substituting 'in the name of the Lord Jesus Christ' for 'through Jesus Christ our Lord.' He asked for all the family to be present and read the prayers with pauses for silence between them. Afterwards one of the women-folk commented to his wife in the kitchen, 'Now we can go to the temple.' What was the background to this remark? It is a universal belief that any contact with death is defiling. If the family cat brings a dead mouse into the kitchen do we not hesitate to pick it up with our fingers? And is our hesitation merely a matter of hygiene? In Hindu thought, if there is a death in the family every member is defiled by it, even if, as in this case, they live thousands of miles away from the place where the death occurred. Until the appropriate rituals of purification are performed the family remain defiled, and so excluded from worship in the temple.

In an urban situation far from home the rituals are likely to be attenuated in any case, but it is also likely to be difficult to find the appropriate ritual specialist unless he is already there to serve a large Hindu community. In his absence a local Christian minister will do instead. Here too some interpretation is needed before passing judgement. Ceremonial purification is not to be dismissed merely as an empty external rite. Of course it may become that, but then so may any rite in any religion. The purification ceremony is a way in which grief can be symbolically expressed and so contained within appropriate boundaries.

These examples of requests made to a minister call for comment of a more general nature. They were all made in a matter-of-fact way and without any trace of hesitation or diffidence. Those who made them assumed that the response

to them would be positive. They were in no doubt that the
minister would do what he was asked to do. Behind this lies
the Hindu assumption that divinity is so to speak diffused
among people in a variety of ways no one of which is in any
way exclusive or definitive. To put it more crudely, one bit of
religion is as good as another, so you make use of what is
available wherever you happen to be. We should note that
this attitude is much less characteristic of Muslims.

The minister therefore can respond to such requests in one
of two ways: he may, as the above argument has suggested,
do what he is asked, but he can never be content merely to do
that. He will always want to do something more, something
which will create the possibility of a growing relationship in
which the original request may eventually come to be seen in
different terms by those who made it.

There is much in the Gospels to support such an approach.
For example when the mothers bring their children to Jesus
for him to touch they no doubt regard him as just another
holy man whose blessing will convey power. It is not Jesus
but his disciples who want to turn them away. Jesus does
much more than he is asked, but, to use the time-honoured
jargon, he begins where people are.

So too with the woman who suffered from an issue of
blood. Her attitude to Jesus borders on the superstitious, but
he refuses to allow her to remain anonymous. He stops, turns
round, asks who touched him, and so establishes a personal
relationship with the woman.

On the other hand a minister who is not convinced by such
arguments may refuse the request on the grounds that to
accede to it would be to blur his witness to the distinctiveness
of Christ if not actually to compromise it. Such a reaction is
certainly theologically defensible but it imposes on him the
duty to explain why he is refusing. That explanation, if it is
made with patience and with charity, can itself become the
foundation for a growing relationship.

So far we have looked at specific requests which may be
made to the minister as his loitering begins to bear fruit.
Slowly he is not only getting to know others but is himself
being known and recognized. As other people invite him into
their homes and so into their lives he finds himself listening
to their questions and problems. Young people may not want

to marry the partners chosen by their parents. A family, or a whole community, may be worried about events in their country of origin. There are the problems of sickness and unemployment, of growing up and growing old. He may well find himself increasingly valued as counsellor and friend. Opportunities of speaking about Christ are likely to be rare, but he can always speak *from* Christ, that is in words which are Christian in spirit and intent.

He will quickly come to realize that the individuals and families he meets belong to communities. Not only are these groups very different from one another, they are no more internally united and monolithic than Christians. Care is needed here. Muslims stress their common brotherhood and do not like to be asked, on first acquaintance, about the divisions within their ranks. Sikhs, if asked which of the local gurdwaras they attend, will often reply that they are not attached to any particular one. Are not we ourselves embarrassed if the first question a person of another faith asks us is about the divisions between Christians? Besides the main religious groupings there are a number of new religious movements springing up which often have their roots in Hinduism and Sikhism.[2]

Asians will mostly have their own centres for worship and assembly, and this brings us back to the mosques, temples and gurdwaras to which reference has already been made. The minister will naturally want to meet his 'opposite number', the imam, granthi or priest, but he will need to be careful not to assume that their function is similar to his own. He will probably discover that they are the paid ritual specialists of their community. Real power is vested in the committee which runs the place of worship. There is nothing corresponding to the parson's freehold. Nor is there any kind of training comparable to his own. The imam or granthi will probably know much of the sacred scriptures by heart but will have strikingly little general knowledge. He will not have received anything comparable to a liberal education. At the same time he is likely to be very direct and self-confident in speaking of his own faith.

Conversations are apt to seem paradoxical occasions. There may be a genuine and growing friendship—a meeting of hearts—while minds seem very far apart from one another.

Also, the idea of studying another religion with objective sympathy, without actually intending to join it, is a western notion of recent origin, probably going back to the Enlightenment. So the minister should not be surprised if his own enthusiasm to ask questions about the other religion is not reciprocated. By the same token he should not be disappointed if his visits to other places of worship are not returned either.

All that we have suggested so far is an unstructured, opportunist kind of ministry. This is indispensable for building up trust and confidence, for it is fundamentally about loving people as they are for their own sakes, and so about being interested in them, in their daily lives, and in their religions.

Some relationships will grow, some will wither or get stuck. The minister will need to be realistic about this, so that he can devote his time and energy to nourishing growth, yet he must also beware of giving people the impression that he has dropped them and is no longer interested in them. This can be deeply wounding to people who themselves may be much less secure as people than he is. One way of avoiding this is to be realistic about the number of people with whom he can keep in touch. To know a few people really well is much more fruitful than dashing about trying to spend a short time with a large number.

But by this time his ministry has grown beyond the preliminary stages and some fundamental decisions will have to be made about its scope and direction.

We have underlined the importance of an unstructured beginning to this type of ministry, but an unstructured ministry has one great weakness: everything is invested in one person and there is no provision for continuity when he has gone. So, does he set up a new structure, or does he join one which already exists? More important than this question is the matter of timing. It is of vital importance not to raise the question of structure too soon. At this point the minister needs to be honest about his own particular gifts and temperament. Some people are happier and more effective in committees and organizations than in the kind of ministry which we have so far described. It may be easier to attend a meeting than actually to meet people. It may be easier to do battle for one's neighbour's rights than actually to get to know him and love him as a person. It is tempting to be vociferous about the evils of racism and to make this a substitute for the costly business of getting to know people of different origins. That is why, for his own good, the minister needs always to keep an unstructured element in his ministry in the way we have described. The structures must be built on this foundation and not made to serve as a compensation for failure to have any foundation at all.

But what kind of structure? There are a number of possible options. The minister may decide to join the local Community Relations Council. These councils were set up in several parts of the country in the sixties with the laudable and appropriate intention of working for racial harmony. Christians and others of liberal persuasion were often active in setting them up and in serving on them in these early years. Now however most of the Asian communities are well established and have their own organizations, religious and political. They are well able to represent themselves. However, their communities are often fragmented and divided. Effective power in the CRC may be vested in a small number of people. Other Asian groups and sometimes people of Afro-Caribbean origin often feel left out and denied access to such power as the CRC may have. Local white people often think that the CRC is concerned with the narrowly communal interests of the Asian groups who have power within it, and that it is not concerned with the welfare of the whole local community. Yet the CRC may be the only available outlet for Asians who have a legitimate political ambition.

All this may do very much less than justice to the work of the CRCs in many areas. For our purposes the point is not whether these complaints are true: the fact is that they are widely made, and the minister who is considering entering this particular field of activity needs to be very clear about what he is doing. He needs to place his feet with care and foresight.

CRCs are properly concerned with racial justice, with issues of power and prejudice. These concerns can sometimes generate a kind of political language which enables its users to speak of one important dimension in the local scene but which ignores others. In some parts of the country racial attack and harassment are tragically commonplace, in other areas racial prejudice is so to speak just below the surface of life, and probably in all of us it is much more deeply rooted in our unconscious attitudes than we realize. But in some parts of the country the issues which really concern Asians in their daily lives are those within and between their own communities and not those at the interface with the white community. No less important, the minister's friendship with ordinary Asians in homes, shops and on the streets will give him a natural grape-vine which can enable him to judge how much support a local leader really has among the people he represents, and how far the issues he raises in public correspond to what his own community really believes to be important.

Alternatively, the minister may decide to join or to start an interfaith group. Such groups now exist in many parts of the country and so plenty of experience is available. Sometimes they consist of members officially appointed by the various communities. More often they consist of people who choose to join, so that the group functions in an unofficial way. At their best these groups afford a forum for members of different religions to understand and appreciate one another's faiths, and to discuss matters of common concern, such as the religious education of children in our kind of society, marriage, and so on.

To be effective such groups usually depend on three factors. They need to operate in a fairly small area where communication is easy and public transport readily available. Secondly, at their heart is nearly always one person, usually a Christian, who is prepared to undertake the chores involved in running any organization, and more than that, who enjoys the confidence of all members of the group. Third, the existence of such a group depends on a sufficient number of people who can speak English with confidence and fluency and who can be articulate about their own religion. This means there is usually a certain middle-class aura to the enterprise. The danger of such groups is that with the passage of time they can too easily become coteries of people who are deeply committed to one another, but who have not discovered ways of feeding back their experience to the communities to which they belong. Indeed their communities may be deeply suspicious of what they are doing.

Again, this is by no means to condemn or despise such groups, it is to point out that the minister who joins one or who decides to set one up should be aware of what he is doing. He is not a well-meaning amateur but a professional, and part of his professionalism is to be aware of these issues.

Notes

1. For a fascinating, moving and important account of what can happen when face-to-face contact is established, see Donovan, V., *Christianity Rediscovered.* SCM 1978.
2. See Appendix C.

THREE

The Role of the Local Church

The minister is in some way linked to a Christian congregation and it is now time to explore this relationship in more detail. The constitutional arrangements are important, for these will affect the way in which he and the congregation perceive one another. At the same time they will define the boundaries of his work, imposing limits, and creating opportunities.

Three kinds of relationship are possible: he may be a specialist who has perhaps served in India, Pakistan or Bangladesh, and has some knowledge of the background, religion, culture and language of a particular Asian group. Asians have enough in common for this knowledge to be of value in a context wider than that of the particular group from which he has gained it. Such a person may be appointed not to a parochial charge, but to a deanery or diocese. This means that his experience is available to the Church in a wide area and not locked away in a particular parish. Also, being free from parochial responsibilities he has plenty of opportunity for developing relationships with the local Asians in the ways which we suggested in chapter 2.

However, this kind of arrangement carries with it two dangers: first, clergy, like any other professional group, have an entirely natural and proper suspicion of specialists who are not doing a 'normal' job in a normal way. Their confidence has to be won: it cannot be taken for granted. The specialist is therefore in a different position from a new incumbent who fits into a well-known category. Second, the specialist is likely to find he has plenty of time to develop relationships with Asians during the first year or two of his ministry, but as he becomes more widely known he will be increasingly called on by local Christians, towards whom indeed he has a most important teaching ministry. For his aim must always be not to keep his expertise to himself, but to share it as widely as possible. Yet if he is not careful he will find himself spending all his time talking about ministry to people of other faiths and none in actually meeting them himself. Here is yet another example of that tendency which we described in chapter 2.

However, in the nature of things this kind of appointment is rare and in any case this book is not primarily written with such people in mind.

In the second kind of arrangement the minister is appointed to a parish or to a team in the usual way, but by arrangement with the bishop and Parochial Church Council a certain proportion of his time is allotted to ministry to people of other faiths. Here too, because this is an unusual arrangement, the confidence of local Christians has to be won. Moreover the situation will not be static and one side of the ministry — usually the church one — will be increasingly likely to swamp the other.

The third arrangement is the most common and the one which we have mainly in mind in writing this book. The minister feels he ought to meet the local Asians, or else he finds himself drawn willy nilly into ministry among them, simply because they are there and so is he. For example:

> It began the day we moved in. As the removal van drew up, children and adults appeared as if from nowhere and helped to carry furniture and fittings into our new home. And we had met none of them previously. Afterwards we went round to express our thanks. Their welcome was overwhelming, and soon we were talking like old friends; even our lack of Urdu and their limited English only added to the fun. Since then we have sampled one another's traditional foods, exchanged gifts, shared in parties and discussed the similarities and differences we'd noticed about our separate faiths.[1]

As the minister becomes more deeply involved he has to ask himself how he can carry his congregation with him. He needs not only their understanding but also their endorsement for what he is doing. Further, if there is to be any continuity after he has left, he needs to find ways of encouraging and enabling some of them to be involved as well.

If that is to become possible he must first win their

confidence on other grounds. We can only win people's confidence by listening to them. We are all willing to trust someone if we know they have given us the whole of their attention, and truly heard both what we have said and what we have left unsaid. Leadership then depends on being able to articulate people's deepest intuitions in ways that they could not do for themselves. When our leaders do this in the areas of our lives with which we are familiar, we are willing to trust them when they take us into strange territory.

As the minister listens to his people he will discover how they see the area in which he works. They probably see it as being in decline. Local industries will have been badly hit by the recession and the younger and more vigorous members of the white community will probably have left in order to find a living elsewhere. Houses will be dilapidated, many of the roads in need of repair, and the social services stretched beyond their capacity to cope with local need. It is very likely too that the area suffers not just from economic decline but from a loss of civic identity. Instead of enjoying a measure of independence, with its own mayor and council, it may be a small part of a much larger metropolitan borough to which it has no historic or emotional ties. People's sense of hurt and loss is usually focused on some external symbol—the High Street for example. They can probably remember the days when there used to be flourishing and elegant shops on either side of it, but now these have gone.

All this can be learnt in asides from conversations which are actually about other things, but they will enable the minister to build up in his mind a picture of how his congregation see both their past and their present. The sense of decline and loss is matched by a decline in self-confidence and self-esteem. Few of the congregation are likely to have the inner resources which might enable them to take or respond to new initiatives. Most of those who still live in the area are likely to be elderly, while other members probably moved away some years ago, their membership of the Church being their one remaining link with the area.

It is against this background that the congregation are likely to perceive those who have moved in from other countries over the last twenty years. More detailed impressions will largely depend on how much and what kind of genuine personal contact with the in-comers they have had. If they have had none at all or very little then their over-all impression is likely to be negative.

For example, an Asian in the milk business disturbs his neighbours by moving bottles about in the early morning. The Asian shop-keepers in the High Street display their wares by putting them in boxes on the pavement, but 'in the old days there was a line of bricks set into the pavement and no-one was allowed to put anything beyond that line — but today no-one takes any notice of that bye-law.' Moreover, 'the shops stay open all hours and they are manned by the whole family, so they do not have to pay wages to assistants as white shop-keepers do.'

Sometimes white and Afro-Caribbean parents of school children resent the provision of mother-tongue teaching for Asian children, believing that this gives the latter an unfair advantage.

A public house is bought by an Asian. A white customer who has long patronized it finds that the old British queue system has disappeared and as a result he now has to wait much longer to be served. He feels that another small but to him significant part of his environment has been eroded. It is also more than likely that one or two church buildings in the area are now gurdwaras, mosques or temples. That too adds to the sense of unease.

'I wish they would try to speak English', is another complaint which can sometimes be heard. For to hear a group of strangers talking in a language one cannot understand is a strangely unnerving experience. Sometimes indeed white people can be heard to say: 'We are strangers in our own country.'

These are all genuine examples taken from a number of different places: they concern neither race nor religion but culture. It is strange *behaviour* that the indigenous inhabitants find difficult to accept. This attitude is usually found alongside an almost total ignorance of what the various Asian communities actually believe and live by.

No doubt there is an element, perhaps a strong element of racism in these attitudes, but to condemn people for this reason is both superficial and futile. People living in declining city areas feel a deep sense of deprivation and hurt, and a consequent insecurity. It is this problem which must be tackled first. Only those who are secure in themselves can dare to think positive thoughts about strangers, and dare to meet them in a positive and loving way.

The minister's next task, therefore, is to interpret what his congregation tell him by placing it in a wider context than they themselves can provide. This he can do because he comes to the area as an outsider. He may feel that this fact sets him at a disadvantage, because he wants above all to belong, to identify with his people. Yet he can never fully do this for he cannot shed his background, his education and the security which these things have given him. He needs to recognize the benefits of being a 'foreigner'. It means, or should mean, that he is well aware that the scene in Britain's inner city areas is but one example of what has been happening in the rest of Europe and indeed in many other parts of the world during the last thirty years. Political changes, springing initially from the end of empire, and technological changes which enable both people and ideas to travel further and faster than they have ever done before — these factors together with the economic ones account for the coming of the Asians and others to this country. Their arrival is in no way a cause of the decline for which they are often made the scapegoats.

To enable his people and others in the area to set their own hurts and discontents in this wider framework is an important part of the minister's role. In order to be able to maintain it he needs to preserve a measure of detachment. If he becomes so totally identified with the area that he begins to share the attitudes of those who live in it then he has surrendered the value of his 'foreignness'. He also needs to know something of the history of the place. Did other immigrants settle there in the past? If they did, how did local people react to them? In some parts of Britain it was the Irish and the Jews who moved in a few generations back. The same derogatory remarks which some white people make today about people of Asian or Afro-Caribbean origin were made by their parents and grandparents about these earlier arrivals.[2]

This points to the obvious fact that every society has its scapegoats. In India they are the outcaste groups, in Japan the Burakumin. There is a strange irony here: people try to secure their own identity by putting others beneath them in the social hierarchy—yet that is simply to repeat what other groups of people have always done and still do the world over. In other words, whenever 'we' try to prove that we are superior to 'them' our very attempt simply betrays the fact that we are no different from anyone else.

To show that our culture is relative to others in this way is an important element in ministry to those who are imprisoned behind inadequate and prejudiced attitudes.

To understand how his people see their area, and then to set what they see in this wider context are the two primary elements in the minister's responsibility towards the congregation. Nor are they tasks which are ever completed. He needs to go on working at them all the time.

Next, he needs to discover what individual members of the congregation are doing to relate to their Asian neighbours in positive ways.

A man may find a friendship developing with an Asian work-mate. A school teacher is invited to the wedding of a pupil's elder brother or sister. Very often it will be the old ladies in the congregation who enjoy the best relationships. They have plenty of time on their hands, and the Asian neighbours next door can fill a real gap in their own lives. The neighbours' children can be surrogate nephews, nieces and grandchildren, and welcoming them can be the best way into a real relationship with their parents.

One such old lady finds herself living with a Sikh and a Muslim family on either side of her: 'They don't speak to each other, but I am on the best of terms with both of them. I wouldn't live anywhere else in the world.'

Another tells of how the Asian mother next door confides in her: 'I had an arranged marriage myself but I don't want that for my own children, I want them to be able to choose for themselves.'

Sometimes a friendship can begin in an unexpected way: some Sikhs moved into the house next door to one lady. For a long time she never spoke to them nor they to her. Then one night she heard a noise outside her front door. She peeped through the sitting room curtains and there she saw one of her neighbours trying, as she thought, to break into her house. Terrified, she phoned the police who came round at once. They asked the neighbours what was going on and soon were able to reassure the old lady. One of the Sikhs had arrived home drunk after a wedding party and had been trying to open her front door instead of his own. So there was nothing for her to be alarmed about.

The police departed but the old lady felt thoroughly ashamed of herself. Next morning she rang her neighbours' door bell for the first time and told them she had come to apologize for calling the police. The family invited her in, gave her a cup of tea, and from that moment became firm friends. When, after a few years she became too infirm to do her own shopping, they did it for her. They would call the doctor when she was ill and generally took care of her.

Sometimes the elderly—like anyone else—can make a deeper impact on other people than they either realize or intend. A Hindu doctor, a geriatric specialist, once approached an Indian Christian living in this country and said: 'I want to learn more about Jesus.' The Christian asked him why and the doctor replied: 'It's all those old people in the hospital where I work. I notice such a difference between those who are Christians and those who are not. The Christians are quiet and contented. They are good patients. They read their Bibles and say their prayers, and when they die it's always with some kind of hope. The others all die in despair.'

But while such positive stories are true they are not the whole truth and we must not romanticize. Others are far less happy: there are only a few 'white' houses left in a street and the Asian neighbours say to the old lady who has lived there all her life: 'This road belongs to us now. You sell us your house and go.'

The other people who seem to relate best to their Asian neighbours are those who are themselves immigrants. Perhaps they have actually lived abroad, or at any rate they have moved into the area from elsewhere. The experience of uprooting oneself and moving means that less of one's sense of personal identity is invested in the new place. Perhaps too one is less worried at what other people may think. It is always easier to be adventurous away from home. An Indian Roman Catholic priest working in the Hindu holy city of Varanasi (Benares) in North India once remarked that he found it comparatively easy to meet Hindus there, but whenever he went back home on holiday to Kerala, fifteen hundred miles away to the south, and saw the Hindu temple at the end of the street where his home was, 'all the old antagonisms arise in my heart.'

The positive stories, then, do need to be seen against a more sombre background, but if that is done, they can be collected and used. It is humbling for the minister to discover what other people are doing — and will go on doing whether he is there or not. He is not alone and it is a kind of arrogance for him to think that he is. The stories can also serve to encourage other people to go and do likewise. They touch the imagination and make the hearers think: 'I could do that too.' This is far more effective than pulpit exhortations to virtue which can only make the hearers feel guilty and inadequate, and so serve to separate the minister from his people.

But there is or can be more to the stories than this, for the idea of theology as story is enjoying something of a vogue today. It has rich possibilities for the kind of situations we are discussing in this book. Let us consider what some of these possibilities are.

Every community, like every individual, lives by a story. The story I can tell of my life defines my identity. It tells me — and others — who I am. If I am to be a whole and integrated person my story must go on. If it stops then I stop growing. I become the bore whom everyone else avoids because all I want is an audience to whom I can repeat the story of the past. In some cases I may actually have a breakdown, for if my story comes to an end I have no meaning. A community can also break down and disintegrate for similar reasons.

If this is not to happen, everything I do or suffer must be made part of my story. Anything left outside will fester and eventually poison me, for it will be a piece of experience of which I can make no sense. That is why wounds need to be healed and sins forgiven, for only in that way can they be made part of the story, and only if the story continues can I live fully and effectively in the present moment.

Yet very often new elements cannot be fitted into the story. In that case the story itself has to be retold in such a way that they can. The key to future growth is to be found in some element of experience which I have ignored because it seemed too trivial, or which I thrust aside because it was too painful.

It is possible to read the Old Testament in this way. The Hebrew people had constantly to retell their story, incorporating experiences such as invasion and exile and the destruction of Jerusalem which when they happened seemed to make that story totally meaningless. We can also appeal again to the walk to Emmaus and read it in the same way. The life and identity of the two disciples was bound up with the story of their community: 'We had hoped he would have been the one to set Israel free.' The stranger listens to their tale of woe and then shows them that the very thing they had rejected, the idea of a suffering Messiah, was in fact the key to the whole. In other words by reinterpreting their story Christ enabled them to hope. Only so could it find new meaning and so continue.

The minister may well come to see that this healing of memories — of individuals and of the community — is the underlying theme of all his pastoral work, and that it holds all the other elements together. In our context this means that to include the Asians and other immigrants (and their children who are not to be called immigrants because they were born here) is the only way in which the story can go on. White Christians have to come to terms with their presence here and accept them for what they are. A congregation which refuses to do this, or does not recognize that it must, can only in the end wither and perish.

We can reach the same conclusion by a slightly different route if we look at a familiar passage from the Sermon on the Mount.

> You have learned that they were told, 'Love your neighbour, hate your enemy.' But what I tell you is this: Love your enemies and pray for your persecutors; only so can you be children of your heavenly father, who makes his sun to rise on good and bad alike, and sends the rain on the honest and the dishonest. If you love only those who love you what reward can you expect? Surely the tax-collectors do as much as that. And if you greet only your brothers what is there extraordinary about that? Even the heathen do as much. There must be no limit to your goodness as your heavenly Father's goodness knows no bounds.

Normal human behaviour is to love and so to greet those who are like oneself, and in our context that means those who are of the same race, culture and religion. But the followers of Jesus are those who are summoned to transcend these limits because they worship a Father whose love, like the sun and the wind, is unbounded.

Asians are hardly the 'enemies' or 'persecutors' of white people, but very often they are *felt* to be a menace, an alien intrusion into a familiar and beloved place which is made to seem strange because of their coming. To greet them is to turn them from abstractions into people, and from enemies into friends. Such meeting begins to make *shared* memories a possibility, and without shared memories there can be no common life, only a collection of ghettos where all feel threatened by those who are outside their own increasingly constricted boundaries. To greet the stranger is also the best possible way to recover 'lost' territory, for when my enemies have become my friends our territory is shared.

The minister and his people also need to remember that Asians have their own hopes and expectations too. To ignore them would be to make this chapter of the book a none too subtle exercise in patronizing condescension.

An Asian lady commented bitterly on the elderly white people who live in her neighbourhood: 'They will talk to their dogs and cats, but not to us, but we too are human beings.' Many Asian men worked hard and for long hours over many years after they arrived in this country. Unemployment has deeply wounded their self-respect, and in many cases shattered their dream of making a new life. Some find compensation for this in a more assiduous practice of their ancestral religion, and a return to its outward symbols. All this can afford a measure of protection from the harsh world outside.

Others have prospered financially and economically but find that their old religion can no longer speak to their need. They may drift into secular materialism and end up, with a strange reversal of Paul's well known testimony, 'as having everything and possessing nothing'—like so many of their white counterparts. Others join one of the new religious movements which are springing up and in many cases growing rapidly. Most of these movements stress the importance of inwardness and of meditation, while playing down or eliminating altogether the significance of the outward symbols of culture and religion. They offer their members a sense of fellowship and belonging, and much more besides.[2]

To say even this much about Asian expectations may be presumptuous, to say more would certainly be so, for they can and must speak for themselves. Yet one thing more we can say with confidence: what most of them long for is respect and esteem from white people. Sometimes they get it, but often they do not, and a single unhappy experience can drive a person back into their shell.

Nor is this only true of Asians: one of us once attended a day conference designed to help people with normal hearing to be more sensitive to the needs of the deaf. A deaf woman spoke in her sign language through an interpreter. She told us of how she had had meningitis as a baby and so lost her power of hearing. Slowly and painfully, and thanks to the infinite patience of her teachers, she learnt to speak — not perfectly but with reasonable clarity.

When she was sixteen her mother sent her to the baker's shop to buy a loaf of bread. There was a queue in the shop and when she got to the head of it she tried to say: 'Please give me a loaf of bread.' The shop assistant could not understand what she was saying and, of course, did not know she was deaf. Utterly humiliated the girl left the shop in confusion, and from that day could never again summon the courage to speak in public. No doubt the shop assistant was wholly oblivious of what had happened. But such an incident, trivial to those who observe it, yet utterly shattering to the person concerned, can drive someone back into a private or communal world from which they never again dare to emerge.

'All real living is meeting,' wrote Martin Buber, and how profoundly right he was, yet how fragile and tenuous are the threads which join us to one another, and how easily are they snapped.

Yet it is of little use to exhort people to greet their neighbours if they have never done it. The minister needs to set up occasions where people from different communities can meet one another in a setting where all can feel reasonably secure. One obvious and well tried way to start is to take a party of Christians to a local place of worship belonging to another faith. This experience can touch the imagination. A lady visiting a Sikh temple for the first time during One World Week whispered to her neighbour: 'I used to think they should all be sent back where they came from, but when you see them here it's different isn't it?'

A church women's group invited someone who had spent some years in India to come and talk about Indian weddings. Instead of speaking herself she took with her a newly married Sikh girl from the area who spoke about her own wedding. So delighted were the group that they asked her to come again. She for her part was no less delighted to find a group of white Christians who were genuinely interested in her and her customs. After the second visit she invited them to visit the gurdwara, which they did.

During another One World Week some Asian ladies were invited to come and show the members of a church ladies' group how to cook Indian food. They were only willing to come because a 'bridge-builder' had slowly won their confidence over a period of three years. A merry time was had by all, because of course, learning to cook can be a relaxing kind of exercise. People are looking, not at one another, but at something else which interests them all and is not controversial. During the course of the demonstration one of the Christians said to one of the visitors: 'Now when we see you in the street we shall be able to say hello.'

Again, today many Asian ladies are trying to learn English, but even two or three classes a week will not help them much unless they can have regular practice in using what they have learnt. With a little encouragement and help, elderly white Christians are often willing to give an hour or two to an Asian lady in this way.

In the summer of 1985 the Parochial Church Council of an English village invited a party of about twenty-five Sikh mothers and their children to come and spend the day in the country. The white Christians had never met any Sikhs and the Sikhs had never visited the countryside.

The children were taken to a farm and had rides on a horse. Their mothers admired the beautiful embroidery and other kinds of handwork done by a woman who lived in the village. The Sikhs were invited to tea in Christian homes. The mothers were reluctant to eat what was put before them because they were used to observing strict rules about diet. Their children had no such inhibitions and so in the end nothing was left over except in one house where nothing was eaten at all. This was because two of the Sikh families were unable to come at the last minute. The result was that one of the Christian ladies found that she had no guests to eat the food she had so carefully and lovingly prepared. But on the return visit she was delighted to find that two of the Sikh families wanted her to be their guest, and one of the Sikh ladies put her arms round her and embraced her.

That particular story has not yet come to an end. At the time of writing those who had shared in the adventure were still talking about it to their friends and neighbours who were hoping they could be included next time.

Are such incidents to be described as dialogue, witness, service, evangelism or what? The answer is that we do not yet know, and indeed to give them a name too soon, to attempt to control them and make them manageable by putting them safely away into our familiar categories could almost be a kind of unbelief. Has not the Church always wanted a safe and manageable doctrine of the Holy Spirit?

Stories such as this are the raw material for our theology, which must be of such a quality that it enlarges our awareness instead of cramping it, allowing these stories to continue, and enabling others to begin.

Notes

1. *With People of Other Faiths in Britain* (URC 1980), pp. 46—7.
2. Adams, C., *'They Sell Cheaper and They Live Very Odd'* (Community and Race Relations Unit of the BCC 1976), p. 7.

FOUR

Models for Ministry

Every minister has to live in the tension between his own understanding of his role and the expectations which others have of him. He is not alone in this: the doctor, the policeman, the politician, and many others are in a similar position. People expect of them more than they can deliver and often expect the wrong things anyway. This sort of tension is inescapable for anyone who fulfils a public function. Remembering that fact can help the minister to keep himself and his own difficulties in perspective.

But in addition to this there is great confusion today about the role of the minister in a rapidly changing society: this affects all churches. Within the Church of England there is additional confusion about the relationship between stipendiary and non-stipendiary ministries (with 'local' as a further variant), lay-readers and deaconesses. Such confusion can be positive, for the break-down of old and restrictive patterns can open the way for new experiments, greater freedom and a deeper appropriation of the faith. It can also be a temptation: attending endless meetings about new patterns of ministry and their relationship to one another can serve as an unconscious excuse for not engaging seriously with mission. Here, in another form, is the same tendency to which we referred in chapter 2.

All this means that the minister has to get on with his job when his role and its relationship to other roles within the Church is much less clear than he would like it to be. He cannot wait until confusion gives way to clarity, but what he can do in the meantime is to have in his mind a number of different models of what he thinks he should be doing. These can complement and correct one another and so deliver him from allowing any one of them to become an idol, for if this happens neither he nor those whom he is seeking to reach are able to grow. An idol is always a part of a particular reality of which it is falsely believed to be the whole. Thus an idolatrous model of ministry is one which enables the minister to engage only a part of himself with a part of others. This means he cannot truly meet them.

This argument will become clearer if we consider some examples. Chapter 2 contained three implicit models of ministry: the loiterer, the problem-solver and the ritual specialist.

The loiterer 'wastes' time with people. He is only able to do this fruitfully if he 'wastes' time with God in that activity which we call prayer. The person who is open to the mystery of God in prayer can also be open to the mystery of other people. To loiter in streets, homes and shops does enable one to relax. As we have already observed, there are times when every minister has to rush about, and loitering can prevent this from becoming a habit. With practice it can bring back that rhythm of life which gives space for meeting other people and for meeting God. Yet one cannot loiter all the time, for that would be to have a life without boundaries and definition. Loitering only makes sense if it is held in contrast and perhaps in tension with patterns of activity whose rhythms are different.

Our second model was the problem-solver: the man who understands how British officialdom works — in social services, immigration law, housing departments, and job centres. The minister is presumed to have both knowledge and access to power. He knows how the system works and can apply pressure on it at the right point. If he is insecure and uncertain of what he is about he can very easily let this role take him over. Once he starts to run a taxi service to the DHSS or to immigration offices word will quickly get around and he will be inundated with unreasonable demands on his time and energy. He will simply be colluding with the expectations of others, making no demands of them, provoking no questions from them — or from himself. He will simply be encouraging people to be dependent on him for this area of need. In other words, while problem-solving can and should be an element in his ministry he needs to keep it under control and in proportion. This he can only do if he is consciously using other models which can correct it.

The third example was the ritual specialist: demands for this sort of activity are in the nature of things likely to be much less frequent. We have already observed that they are likely to provoke considerable unease in the minister's mind. They are unlikely to 'take him over', indeed he is more likely to reject them altogether. Yet to refuse to meet people at this point of need may be to destroy a relationship. This is why we have argued that such occasions can be seen as opportunities which lead beyond themselves. The question 'What's the matter, didn't you get paid?' is a pointer in that direction.

We now turn to other models which we have not yet considered. Each of them can serve to open up new dimensions to our theme.

First, the minister is often seen as representing more than simply the Christian Church. Other religious groups may also look to him because in their eyes he stands for the tolerance and comprehensiveness of British society. He may find himself invited to other places of worship which are not Christian in order to attend some annual function or civic occasion. His presence is seen as a symbol of the fact that Christians affirm the right of other religious groups to be present in this country, and that therefore they should be allowed the space and freedom to live and worship in their own way. By affirming others in this way he can give them a measure of confidence and this in turn can enable them to meet others on a level of equality, and participate more fully in the wider life of society.

This is not a role which the minister can arrogate for himself, it is one which other groups give him. He will accept it the more readily if he reflects on the history of the Jewish people in this century. To secure the freedom of one religious minority is a step towards securing the freedom of all. At the same time his acceptance may well be tempered with hesitation. How pluralist can society be, and what is it that holds it together? Historically Christianity has made an important if not vital contribution to our sense of national identity and cohesion. People who are half-consciously aware of this may be very uneasy at the thought of the minister attending a function in the local gurdwara, mosque or temple.

When an invitation card arrives in the morning post he has

to reply in a few days. He has no time to work out his position on these vast issues. Perhaps his acceptance — or refusal — will always be attended with a measure of unease.

With the possible exception of the loiterer the models we have considered so far are all based on the assumption that the minister either has power himself or has access to it: as problem-solver he has access to and knows how to manipulate secular power; as ritual specialist he is in touch with sacred power; while as representative he symbolizes the power of the majority community. There is a comic element in all this, for the minister knows perfectly well that he has much less power than those who approach him assume he has, indeed he probably feels himself to be the uncertain representative of a marginalized Church. So let us now consider two models of weakness.

He may consider himself as a clown: in a traditional circus the clown comes into the ring between the acts, to divert the audience while preparations are going on for the next part of the programme. Unlike the juggler, the lion-tamer or the trapeze artist the clown has no obvious skill which it is his business to display. In fact he is very skilled indeed, but the concealment of this fact is part of his art. So too, the minister does not, like the policeman, social worker, or salesman, have any obvious skill, training, or function. To see himself as a clown can shed much light on what he is trying to do. Perhaps, too, clowning and loitering have something in common.

Some examples from situations overseas can serve to illustrate this point.

A missionary teacher in the Sudan had to pay a visit to the local military commander. He duly arrived in his land-rover, parked it alongside several others, had his interview, and then got back into his vehicle to discover that the ignition key would not fit. At which point the commanding officer emerged from his office, saw what was happening and pointed out to the unfortunate missionary that he was trying to start the wrong land-rover: 'That is your vehicle over there. The one you are trying to start belongs to the Sudanese Defence Force.'

There was much hilarity among the soldiers who were looking on but this relaxed the atmosphere. The missionary was invited to lunch and the invitation became a regular daily routine. Why? Because instead of being the omni-competent white man he had now become a figure of fun. No longer perceived as a threat, he was able to become a friend.

The second incident comes from Kenya: a brilliant young athlete from Britain — a middle-distance runner — joined the staff of a school for two years. A few days after he arrived the school had its annual sports day. Everyone was eager to watch the new member of staff show his paces, but neither he nor they had reckoned with the combined effects of heat and jet-lag. He was soundly beaten and in fact 'lapped' by several members of the primary school who were about half his size. The spectators thought this was a huge joke and so, happily, did the athlete. At once the school took him to its heart and he found himself completely accepted by everyone.

The third story comes from West Africa and happened some thirty years ago, when many schools were still run almost entirely by British missionaries. There was a girls' school with high standards of professional excellence and of Christian dedication and care. One day the head-mistress received a cable from England telling her that her father had suddenly died. A few minutes later one of the girls came into the office and found her crying. She put her arm round her shoulders and tried to comfort her. After this incident the whole atmosphere in the school was strangely different, for now the girls had discovered that the missionaries too were equipped with tear ducts and sometimes needed to use them.

Each of these stories contains a moment when someone perceived to have power, status or ability was suddenly and unexpectedly brought down to the normal level of humanity and made either into a figure of fun or an object of compassion. Such moments cannot be engineered or contrived, they can simply be accepted when they come and taken as opportunities, instead of occasions for embarrassment. Such an attitude is not far removed from Paul's use of the words poverty, weakness and folly in the Corinthian correspondence: 'Yet to shame the wise God has chosen what the world counts folly, and to shame what is strong, God has chosen what the world counts weakness. He has chosen things low and contemptible, mere nothings, to overthrow the existing order' (1 Cor. 1.27 — 8).

Paul is writing here of the Christian community in Corinth, but he says much the same thing about his preaching: 'which does not rely on the language of worldly wisdom, so that the fact of Christ on his cross might have its full weight' (1 Cor. 1.17); and about his own experience: 'I shall therefore prefer to find my joy and pride in the very things that are my weakness; and then the power of Christ will come and rest upon me' (2 Cor. 12.9).

In other words, the social composition of the community, the language of preaching, and the nature of spiritual experience are all seen in terms of the cross, which in its reversal of human norms has about it an element of holy clowning. This is a note which is struck in John 19.2−3: 'The soldiers plaited a crown of thorns and placed it on his head, and robed him in a purple cloak. Then time after time they came up to him, crying 'Hail, King of the Jews!' and struck him on the face.' Here Christ in his powerlessness is deliberately made into a figure of fun, yet the meaning of that moment does not lie in the hands of the soldiers, it is determined by what Christ himself does with it.

The same theme can be seen in the Beatitudes, where the kingdom is promised to the poor, the sorrowful, the meek and the persecuted. The very meaning of kingly rule is tranformed, for the conditions here set for its exercise are such as would normally deny its possibility. So too, the person who turns the other cheek and goes the second mile has seized the initiative from the oppressor. Now it is the victim who determines the real meaning of what is going on.

Here we glimpse the strange paradox of the power of love, which can perhaps only truly be released in these moments of weakness and failure whose meaning has been transformed.

Yet if we try to apply this to our theme we face a formidable dilemma: in many parts of the United Kingdom the Anglican Church is still the most dominant religious group. It belongs to a nation which till recently was, and often likes to think it still is, a significant power in the world. How can the members of such a church become figures of weakness in the eyes of other religious groups, except in ways which are contrived and artificial?

This question is not so intractable as it might seem, for in many of the main areas of Asian settlement the Church is largely made up of 'the left behind'. Congregations are mainly elderly, for many of their younger and more vigorous members moved out twenty or twenty-five years ago as the Asians moved in. Often most church members live outside the parish but continue to attend the church which is the one remaining link with the place where they used to live. Then too, Asians have watched with bewilderment, and even with pain, the decline of the churches in recent years. 'Why do so few people attend your churches?' is a question they will often ask. Sometimes the point will be made more forcibly: 'Don't you Christians teach your children anything? How can we bring up our own children properly in such a godless environment?' 'There is too much liberalism. Your people have given up their religion and lost their identity.'

If the minister is prepared to admit to the weakness of the Church without making excuses and without being defensive, than that very admission can perhaps make the weakness a redemptive factor. If clergy can find it in them to be more open about this with one another, they may then be able to practise the same kind of honesty with their Asian parishioners.

There is another and more positive step which the minister can take and that is, to attempt to learn one of the Asian languages spoken in his area. No-one can learn a foreign language unless he is prepared to make a fool of himself.

To begin to learn another language is deliberately to put oneself into a position of weakness over against the community which speaks it. We learn our mother tongue as we grow up, and so to try and learn another is to return to childhood and impotence. It also makes us dependent on the authority of our teacher. That is why the learning process can be so disturbingly humiliating. Anyone who has travelled overseas in some area where no-one can speak English knows what this means. Communication is reduced to a few phrases half-grasped and mispronounced, taken from the tourist guide-book.

The minister is unlikely to be able to learn much of the other language, for he has plenty of other things to do with his time. But that does not matter, nor does it matter how well or badly he speaks it. The important point is that he is making the attempt. He will find this is appreciated out of all proportion to his success.

Why is this so?

The answer lies in the nature of language itself. We often think of it as a tool, as a means of communication, and so it is, and one can learn a foreign language for that sort of strictly practical reason. But a language is much more than a tool, it is a sacrament of a people's very being. To learn their language is to enter most deeply into what they are. It is hard for the English to grasp this point, because our language has never been under threat, but the Welsh grasp it instinctively for it is part of their own experience. The same goes for all minority communities whose identity is bound up with the preservation of their language. It also applies to Jews and to Muslims, who have to teach Hebrew and Arabic to their children in order to maintain the tradition of worship.

If one can see language in this way, and enter, however superficially, into the poetry, prayer and devotion of another community, then one can begin to meet them at that point where they feel they are most truly and deeply themselves.

But in saying this we have moved beyond the model of the clown and on to another: the explorer. To learn another language is to venture into unknown territory. The man who does that has always had an honoured place in our culture. One only has to think of David Livingstone, Captain Scott, or Sir Edmund Hillary to realize that. And why are space probes called by such names as Mariner, Explorer or Ulysses? So too the scientist who makes new discoveries has, or used to have, a place of similar honour.

Today the image of the explorer is less powerful and evocative than it used to be. It is easy to see why. In terms of geography he has been replaced by the tourist who can travel in comfort more or less wherever he wants to. Also we are, or ought to be, more aware than our forefathers of the devastating effects which the opening of other lands and cultures to the impact of the West has often had. Then too, we are much less confident about the fruits of scientific discovery, and so the scientific community is faced in a new way with the moral implications of what it discovers. Yet these very limitations serve to make the image of the explorer even more appropriate today, as we shall see in a moment. The minister, then, explores the mental and spiritual world of those whom he meets. Even a minimal knowledge of the language will help him on these travels, but if that is beyond him he should not despair. For one thing a whole new generation of Asians is growing up who can speak English as well as he can. For another, he can explore many areas of their life for which he does not need to know the language. These include festivals, places of worship, the links which Asian communities maintain with their places of origin, customs surrounding birth, marriage and death, the ways in which tradition is handed on to the next generation, the way a community understands or even creates its own history, the different kinds of Muslims, Sikhs and Hindus; modern reforming movements which have sprung from them—the list is endless.

The mark of the genuine explorer is that he is endlessly fascinated by everyone he meets and by everything he discovers. To be able to be fascinated by other people in this way is already half-way to loving them. The other half depends on what the explorer actually does with his discoveries. This is the moral dimension of what he does, for he has to face the question: to whom do 'my' discoveries belong?

In India there is a widespread popular myth about the impact of the West: in the nineteenth century western scholars learned Sanskrit, the sacred language of the Hindu scriptures, and so discovered the secrets of radio, television, air travel and the bomb, for long ago Hindu India possessed all these things. This explains the technological superiority of the West. It depends on secrets stolen from the Hindus.

The very absurdity of this myth ought to make us look at it more closely. It speaks of the deep sense of hurt which many third world cultures have suffered and continue to suffer because of the intrusion of the West.

In other words, exploration can easily be corrupted and degenerate into exploitation. Yet this is not inevitable: the early explorers would often exchange gifts with the leaders of the new peoples whom they met. That in principle suggested a relationship of reciprocity, even if later events tragically belied this.

Exploring is redeemed from corruption when the explorer recognizes his obligation to give something in return to the people who welcome him. In our context of ministry he can only give the whole of himself, utterly and without reserve. He does this by actually living in the area, by genuinely loving for their own sakes all whom he meets, and by being concerned for their true welfare in every dimension of their personal and corporate lives.

This he has to express sacramentally in his daily encounters with people, both planned and unexpected. It was once said of William Temple that he might give you only ten minutes of his time, but he would give you the whole of himself.

Yet here too we must not romanticize. The minister needs to be rigorously aware of what is happening to himself: in time he begins to feel at home in the 'country' he is visiting. Its geography becomes familiar. He begins to feel its history on his own pulses. He becomes emotionally involved with the issues the Asian communities feel to be important.

If and when he reaches this point he should pause and reflect on his situation. To use an old-fashioned phrase, he is now in danger of 'going native'. This begins when he finds he can no longer communicate with his own people. He finds they are not interested or cannot understand what he is doing. Anyone who has lived overseas for any length of time is familiar with this difficulty. It is very hard to share with others what one has experienced and discovered, but the attempt to do so must never be abandoned, for that is to cut oneself off from the body of Christ.

The explorer also needs a realistic attitude towards the community he is now coming to know and love. He faces two dangers: first, he may become a romantic. Everything in the other community seems wonderful and church life becomes more and more depressing. Yet he needs only to reflect that however much he is made to feel welcome by the other community, he can never actually be a member of it. He is like the townsman who can enjoy the delights of the countryside because he does not have to make his living in it. He can come and go as he pleases, for he does not have to face the constraints of belonging.

He does feel those constraints in his own community. The congregation has its awkward members with whom he has to cope; so too does every parochial church council. So also do the temple and mosque and their management committees, but because the minister is always a guest he does not have to live with that difficulty. He may sometimes be moved to echo the words of an understandably exasperated missionary in India: 'Thank God for other religions!'. But had that missionary actually experienced the life of other religious communities as a member and not as a welcome guest, could he have said that, even as he did, in jest?

Such romanticism is the more tempting today in that most of us are reacting against our forefathers, who often condemned other religions out of hand: 'The heathen in his blindness bows down to wood and stone.' That negative attitude is still to be found, indeed it can on the face of it claim much support from the Bible. The minister who rejects other religions in this way is unlikely to become an explorer. He sees nothing which fascinates him however much he discovers, but for that very reason he faces our second danger: he who dares not risk loving his enemies is condemned to become like them. This can often happen to those who live close to Islam — especially today, when we hear and read so much of militant Islam and of Islamic fundamentalism. The man who allows himself to become obsessed by the dangers of the Islam he fears and rejects will in the end be taken over by that fear and rejection. His Christianity will take on a harshly rigid and unloving aspect. This is a kind of idolatry. We become like what we worship, but we also become like what we fear and with our conscious minds reject, for all the time we are engaged with it and exposing our unconscious minds to its influence.

In other words, the person who lives in close proximity to another religious community will inevitably be changed by the experience. There is nothing extraordinary about that: we are always changed by those among whom we live, and they by us. The question for the minister is how to hold that change within his life in Christ. Neither romanticism about nor crude rejection of the other faith are adequate responses, but in that case what are? Here we must touch briefly on the theme which will occupy us in chapter 5, how we learn from other faiths.

Let us take the test case of idolatry: on seeing the images in a Hindu temple the minister may be appalled or at least uneasy, for is he not seeing with his own eyes what the Bible so unequivocally condemns? Maybe he is, but before coming to that conclusion his first task is to discover what it is Hindus themselves think they are doing. But which Hindus? He may ask a family whom he meets in the temple, but they have probably not thought about it very much. They are, like many people in all religions when they worship, doing what they have always done. They may be embarrassed to find themselves expected to be articulate about it.

He may then ask the priest, but he may simply be a ritual specialist who is not expected to study or reflect on the significance of what he does. Then too, both the family and the priest may be aware of the criticisms which Christians have made of idolatry. They may reply in a way which will, they half-consciously hope, make their practice more acceptable in the eyes of its Christian critics: 'It's only a symbol, like the cross in your churches.'

Yet provided he is aware of these hazards the minister can, by study and by enquiry, build up an account of the use of images which Hindus find they can endorse. Indeed he may be able to help them understand it better for themselves, for there are always aspects of the life of any community which an outsider can perceive and articulate better than its members.

Once he has formed his picture the minister can then, but only then, apply his Christian critique: Is this in fact what the Bible condemns as idolatry? Whether he answers 'yes', or 'no', or 'maybe' his judgement will be made more profoundly and therefore more sympathetically than it would have been if he had not taken the trouble to explore.[1]

This example can further illuminate the explorer's role: he is continually crossing the frontier into the world of the other community, trying first to make sense of it in its own terms. Then he crosses back and shares what he has discovered with his own people, trying now to make sense of it in the light of his own faith. Although he belongs to one community he finds that he is increasingly accepted by others. In order to be able to cross to and fro he needs to know where he has come from. If he does not he is no longer an explorer, but only a refugee. He is lost. Nor does he become a permanent resident in the 'country' he is visiting, for then too he is not an explorer, but an immigrant.

This kind of exploring has its own dynamic which leads us to consider another model, that of reconciler.

In any situation where people of different communities are beginning to meet each other one finds at the heart of it one or two bridge-builders. Such people are always exposed and vulnerable; theirs is a lonely and costly ministry which few people can understand. For example, some young married Sikh women run an advice centre at the local gurdwara. Because they can speak English fluently and have some of the self-confidence which goes with this they can be 'bridges' to the complex world of British bureaucracy – to job centres, DHSS offices, the local housing department. They can also fill in forms, a symbolic link with that bureaucracy which is of very great importance.

But their very ability makes them different from and therefore suspect in the eyes of many members of their own community. There will be men and perhaps other women who will think and sometimes suggest that really they ought to limit themselves to the roles which tradition assigns to women in their community – cooking meals and bearing children.

In similar fashion the Christian minister who begins to associate with Asians may unwittingly uncover deep fears and insecurities in the hearts of his own people. Some of them may feel and say that his real job is to minister to them, and not to 'waste time' with outsiders. Behind this attitude may be the half-conscious fear that some of the outsiders might eventually become insiders – and then what would happen to the familiar routines and safe relationships of church life?

After serving in India for some years a certain man took up a post as parish priest in an area of Asian settlement. After he had been there for two years one of the congregation ventured the remark: 'When you first arrived we were all afraid you were going to fill the church with Pakis.'

To eat with and to welcome those who in the eyes of others are 'publicans and sinners', to greet those who are not 'our brethren', to love our 'enemies' – those whose very presence is feared or unwelcomed by our own community – such acts and attitudes are the essence of bridge-building and they lie at the heart of the gospel.

Up and down Britain today there are people who are daring to venture into this new and uncharted area of ministry. Again and again one finds that they are lonely, isolated and often suspect in the eyes of their Christian friends. Where are they to discover the understanding, encouragement and support which they need?

Further, the bridge-builder, or reconciler, longs to bring together those whom he loves but who never meet one another. In chapter 3 we considered several examples of how this can be done. This needs to be set against another aspect of his ministry. He may find that he is on the best of terms with some of the local Muslims and Sikhs for example, but that none of them meet each other. Part of his role may then be to challenge the stereotypes which many members of these communities have of one another. This points to a creative tension which is of vital importance in many other areas of his activity. He longs to be accepted and welcomed, but if his presence never provokes unease or questions in the minds of his friends, then how can he truly be a sacrament of the presence of Christ?

Any Christian who spends time with Asians in the ways that we have suggested will find that again and again his fellow Christians ask him the same question: 'Are you trying to convert them?'

English is a subtle language where much can be conveyed by nuance and emphasis. So too with this question. It may mean one of several different things: 'I think you really should be trying to convert them, but I suspect you are not really trying hard enough.' That comment is often made from outside the situation. The person who makes it may be rather like the member of the parochial church council who asks why more members of the youth club do not come to church. To this the leader of the club can properly reply: 'If some members of the PCC were prepared to come and spend time with the youngsters, playing snooker and table-tennis, and being willing to chat, then a few of them might see the point.'

But the question may mean the opposite: 'I don't think you should be trying to convert them, but I suspect that you are, and that fact corrupts all your attempts at friendship, for they are made with that ulterior motive.' Behind that comment lies the belief that friendship and love must be offered for their own sakes, without the intention of using them for any purpose outside themselves. That is surely a valid and indeed a necessary point. There are endless opportunities for love and service of our neighbours of other faiths. Some Christians would argue that our task is to take these opportunities, but no more.

Yet here we are faced with a false polarity the germ of which is contained in the form of the original question: the words 'try to convert' give the game away. They suggest that conversion is something which one person somehow does to another, and this savours of manipulation. Since the historic role of the Church of England has been largely pastoral the whole issue has been ignored. The result is that those who think they know what conversion is often have a very restricted understanding of it. Others react against this and reject the notion altogether.

This is how false polarities usually arise and as so often happens the two extremes are based on the same fallacy. In this case both views assume that what will happen in the life of another person or community is what the Christian thinks ought to happen, or can try to make happen. But does this correspond to anyone's experience of life? Surely not.

This brings us by a slightly different route to a point we reached in chapter 2. The minister is trying to love people in the name and for the sake of Christ. That love must indeed have its own integrity. If it is 'used' for anything beyond itself it ceases to be love and becomes something else. But like any lover the minister hopes his love will evoke a response. He can neither predict what that response will be, nor control the results which flow from it. To suggest that he can do either is to deny both the freedom of the other person and the reality of the Holy Spirit.

The response may take the form of a question about Christianity: 'Why do you celebrate Easter?' 'When Jesus was crucified did his followers take revenge?' 'What is the difference between Catholic and Protestant?' When such questions are asked the minister is expected to be a spokesman on behalf of Christianity. He has to bear witness to his faith. Indeed he may well be taken aback at the assurance with which some Asians testify to what they live by, which often puts his own diffidence and timidity to shame.

His friends will therefore on occasion expect him to bear witness to the faith that is in him. If he speaks with conviction as he must, there is bound to be an element of persuasiveness in what he says.

Some young Asians in this country have become Christians in recent years. The experiences and reasons leading to their conversion are extraordinarily varied, and church history confirms that this is usually so. There seems to be no guaranteed route to Christian belief, and therefore no single way of presenting the gospel. Often, however, they are attracted by outgoing and vigorous Christian groups which are not directly related to other churches. The causes of this separateness are manifold. For obvious reasons the converts often lack the self-confidence to be at ease in British society. Most of us live surprisingly restricted lives and have a narrow range of friends. We should hardly be surprised if young Asian converts feel they need the company of their own kind. It is important for Christians from the main-line churches to understand and respect this need, while at the same time keeping in touch with these groups to prevent them from becoming ghettos. Indeed the rest of us sorely need their presence and their witness, and our long-term aim can only be a genuinely multi-racial Church. Similar issues arise in relating to congregations of Afro-Caribbean origin. There are some areas where a church whose membership is already black and white is also trying to relate to the local Asian community. This places considerable emotional demands on all concerned, who need more understanding and support from outsiders than they sometimes get.

Converts too are subject to emotional pressures and if they are to cope with these they need the imaginative sympathy —and in practical terms that means above all the *time*—of others. They often face opposition from their families. They need help in exploring their new-found faith and in discovering how much of their former tradition they can retain, what they have to reject, and what elements of it can be 'baptized'. Yet it is possible to speak much too patronizingly of the 'care of converts'. There are few more humbling and enriching experiences than listening to the testimony of one for whom Jesus Christ is a fresh and wonderful discovery. At the same time it is always wrong to make use of converts, by treating them as exhibits to support our own precarious Christian identity.

We have to remember too that people are not only converted to Christianity, they are also converted out of it, to other traditional faiths or to one of the new religious movements which we describe in Appendix C. They too often face opposition from their families, and can sometimes give moving and impressive testimony to their new-found faith. The communities they join are often more multi-racial than the churches — indeed that is part of their attraction.

This implicitly raises profound issues about a Christian theology of religions, and about the meaning of mission and of evangelism. The Church is only slowly beginning to think about these questions, but the minister cannot simply ignore the Asians who live in his parish until the Church has made up its collective mind, if indeed it can ever do so. What we have suggested in this chapter are some models which may enable him to act now with both integrity and conviction. Further, the Church of England will only get its theology right if it listens to those engaged in the kind of ministry we have suggested here.

Notes

1. For a fuller discussion of this issue see Hooker, R. H., *What is Idolatry?* BCC 1986.

FIVE

Learning from Other Faiths

by Roger Hooker

Christians who meet people of other faiths, visit their homes and places of worship, and study what they believe and practise, will often testify that this has been a very rewarding experience, and that their own faith in Christ has been deepened and enhanced as a result. Yet when pressed to be specific and say precisely what it is they have learnt they can often be curiously inarticulate. This may be partly due to the fact that the deepest and most important experiences of life are difficult to put into words anyway, yet their hesitations can often fuel the suspicions of other Christians to whom the whole notion of learning from other faiths savours of syncretism — an attempt to add to Christ that which is incompatible with him in the interests of superficial harmony and cheap compromise. It also seems like a betrayal of the mission which is at the heart of the Christian enterprise. Both parties can often feel that beneath the surface of such disagreement great issues lie hidden.

Patently clarification is needed: one way of achieving this is for one of us to describe and reflect on his own experience of learning, so in this chapter I shall be sharing something of what I have learnt and continue to learn from Hinduism, but before doing so some comments of a more general kind are necessary.

Experience of anything never comes to us in the raw: it is always filtered through the lens of our own presuppositions. We cannot experience anything unless we interpret it and that means we have to have a ready-made frame of reference in which it can be placed, otherwise it remains nonsense, an absurdity.

Our presuppositions are therefore necessary, for without

them we cannot think at all, but at the same time they are ambivalent. Any frame of reference enables us to see certain things clearly, but other things will be distorted, and yet others remain totally invisible. Cartographers are familiar with this phenomenon: any map of the world is a two-dimensional projection of a reality which is three-dimensional. To have a reasonably accurate map of the world no one projection is enough, many are needed. A map therefore is not and cannot be an objective and true description, it is a model and needs to be studied in conjunction with other models. Scientists too recognize that their descriptions are models in this sense. Indeed we might well claim that model-making is the only way we can comprehend reality at all.[1]

So too, to make sense of Hinduism I find I need the help of many different 'map-makers'—historians, psychologists, anthropologists, linguists, to name only a few. Each of these groups can be further subdivided, for like theologians they do not agree among themselves.

Also, I need to bring my own Christian presuppositions to the level of consciousness, recognizing that other Christians, say of Catholic or Orthodox background, will look at Hinduism with eyes which are very different from my own. What I am capable of seeing is limited by my personal history, my sex, my country and culture, my churchmanship and many other factors of which I am unaware. To recognize this state of affairs without embarrassment or disappointment is surely an element in the Christian virtue of humility.

Further, to be able to learn from another faith I need a certain understanding of my own. For me Christianity is primarily a set of relationships into which I am summoned and invited to enter—with God through Christ and with other Christians, living and departed. That fellowship creates the context within which alone Christian language can be spoken and understood. The language is crucial for without it the relationships would be impossible, but it is they which are the more important. Persons and the relationships between them can never be encapsulated in words, though a particular form of words may express them more or less adequately for a particular time and place, and some words carry more weight than others. All Christians would want to give special weight to the words of the Bible and the Creeds (though on how much and what kind of weight there is a wide variety of opinions).

One can put this differently in some words of Leonard Hodgson: 'Christ gave his life: it is for Christians to discern the doctrine.' In other words we are continually searching for new ways in which to describe who Christ is and what he has done for us, new ways of telling the old story. This means that Christianity can never be primarily a set of propositions to which we have to give our assent. Important though that element is, it is always secondary to the relationships.

If that be so then there must always be an open-endedness and incompleteness about Christian discourse. We are always in search of new materials with which we can deepen, enrich and expand what we say about Christ. Indeed modern scholarship discerns such a process within the New Testament itself. It contains not one but many theologies, which express the claims made for the one Christ, crucified and exalted, in different places and at different times. This process has continued throughout history where Christianity has always been something of a hitch-hiker, using local and contemporary forms of thought to express itself on its journey through time, and finding its own understanding of the gospel deepened in the process. A modern example of this can be found in the late Bishop Ian Ramsey's book *Religious Language*.

He describes the purpose of the book, which was first published in 1957, in the following terms:

> Contemporary philosophy lays on us an urgent task and duty, viz. to elucidate the logic of theological assertions, and this book may be seen as an endeavour to face and to measure something of the challenge of contemporary philosophy; to state a case for religious language; to try to elucidate the logic of some of its characteristic claims. Nor is that all . . . I hope to be able to show at the same time the considerable benefits for theological apologetic and controversy which can arise from facing this challenge with which contemporary philosophy presents us.[2]

Ramsey recognized the challenge which contemporary philosophy posed and continues to pose for Christian faith: if the philosophers were right, then Christianity's claims to truth collapsed in ruins. Yet he goes on to say that the facing of the challenge can bring 'considerable benefits for theological apologetic and controversy'. Indeed the whole book is a classic example of the way in which Christians can learn from that which is at the same time a challenge and a threat.

Therefore to suggest that Christians can learn from other faiths is not to propose anything new, still less heretical, it is merely to suggest that they continue to do what, at their best, they have always done in the past. Indeed when they cease to learn from their environment their faith merely ossifies. In his book *Yes to God*[3] Alan Ecclestone powerfully illuminates the poverty of our contemporary Christianity in Britain, a poverty which he traces to, among other things, our neglect of the poets and artists.

Accordingly, to learn from that which is at one level alien and hostile, is not only possible for Christians, it is also essential for the health and survival of the faith.

Yet it is also very disturbing, for that which is alien to ourselves is always perceived as having overtones of menace. We are disturbed by philosophies which deny the possibility or the truth of our own beliefs, by poetry and art which are untraditional and which may seem to be blasphemous, by whole communities which in every conceivable way—dress, diet, language, colour, beliefs and customs—are different from ourselves.

Very often we try to diminish this sense of otherness in order to remove its threat. An alien community may be confined to a ghetto, and so banished to the edges of our awareness. Another religion may be dismissed, without study, as wholly bad, for then there is no need to take it seriously. Alternatively it may be seen as very little different from our own, for if 'they' are really no different from 'us' their presence can no longer be a menace to our own sense of security. Some Indologists and anthropologists take shelter behind the professional limits of their respective disciplines, so that what they study is kept at an emotional distance from themselves.

Yet Christians need to feed on the sources of security which their own faith affords. If they do so then they can dare to live with the otherness of the other faith and so start to learn from it. So the more secure one is in one's own faith, the more one is able to learn from the other.

I now turn to my own personal experience, describing what I have learnt from Hinduism. This happens to be the tradition with which I am most familiar, so what follow are simply examples of what can be done. I describe what I have learnt on an ascending scale. At the bottom end the positive influence of Hinduism is minimal or non-existent — though one must never forget the real and inescapable fact of unconscious influence. At the top end the influence is at its maximum. Put differently, we move up the scale from that which is not threatening at all to that which can be very threatening.

First of all I have learnt a great deal *about* Hinduism in the same way in which I have learnt about a whole host of other things — music, cricket, gardening, history, literature. In any area of life and study one can and does acquire objective knowledge without so to speak taking it into one's being. It is interesting or diverting, but at a conscious level has no profound effect. But when I start to learn *from*, then I am personally affected or even changed.

So in the second place, I learn from Hinduism by way of negative contrast. By this I mean, somewhat crudely, I have experienced or discovered 'bad' things in Hinduism which have illuminated 'good' things in Christianity of which previously I was wholly or partly unaware. The experience of Hinduism as different has helped me to go deeper into my own inheritance.

To quote some examples: I once took a Christian wedding in India at which many of the guests were Hindus. There was bedlam: many of the guests arrived late, they walked in and out of the service. Many of them were talking to one another all the way through and there seemed no attempt to give the occasion their attention. There was a total absence of what I understood by order and reverence.

This experience sent me back to 1 Corinthians 14 where Paul is trying to control the disorderly exuberance of the newly founded Corinthian church. The two cases are not precisely parallel but I found myself reflecting in a new way on his final injunction at the end of that chapter: 'Let all be done decently and in order', and on the theology on which he bases it: 'God is not a God of disorder but of peace.' Did this point to something distinctively Christian which was not to be found within Hinduism?

On another occasion I was talking to a Christian surgeon who was on holiday from Nepal, where he worked at a hospital. He told me of a Hindu villager who had fallen from the branch of a tree made slippery by the rains and broken his arm. Sadly, he had delayed coming to the hospital until gangrene had set in. The surgeon realized he had no choice but to amputate the arm in order to save the man's life. He spent six hours trying to persuade him to allow him to do this, but in vain. The man refused because he believed that unless his body was physically complete he could not enter heaven.

As I listened to my friend I found my mind going back to Matthew 5. 29—30:

> If your right eye leads you astray, tear it out and fling it away; it is better for you to lose one part of your body than for the whole of it to be thrown into hell. And if your right hand is your undoing, cut it off and fling it away; it is better for you to lose one part of your body than for the whole of it to go to hell.

Even allowing for the element of hyperbole in those words, they suddenly revealed an implicit view of human nature and destiny and of the role of our bodies which seemed wholly at odds with the one encountered by my surgeon friend.

A third experience comes from my days as a student of Sanskrit. The wife of one of my teachers gave birth to a son who was born prematurely and seriously deformed. He only lived for a week. The teacher consulted an astrologer to discover why this tragedy should have struck his family. He was told that he had come under the malevolent influence of the planet Rahu, and that to prevent such a terrible thing happening again he should wear a special ring made of seven different kinds of metal. This would protect him from the influence of the planet.

The family, whom I knew well, experienced real grief at what had happened, yet seemed to ask no questions. There was no anguished 'My God why?' such as we find throughout the Psalms, and indeed at the heart of all Christian and Jewish experience of suffering and evil. There was of course a question addressed to the astrologer, but that received a simple and satisfactory answer in a way that the Christian question does not.

This made me reflect in a new way on the Christian understanding of God as the one to whom questions can and must be addressed about the way in which he orders or fails to order our experience for our good.

Here then were three very different experiences of Hinduism, each of which threw into sharp relief a contrasting element in my own faith. Yet on reflection none of them proved to be quite as simple and clear-cut as I had at first assumed: it was impossible to translate them into universal and generalized perceptions about Hinduism and Christianity. To do that I would have needed, in the first example, to conduct a survey of the way in which Hindus behaved at Christian weddings right across India over a long period of time. I might then have discovered significant variations in different parts of the country and among different social groups.

And what about *Christian* behaviour at Christian weddings across the world and throughout history? In other words, how far was what I considered to be reverent and orderly behaviour merely the reflection of my own middle-class Anglo-Saxon background, and how far was it genuinely rooted in the gospel?

So too with the man who presumably died eventually of gangrene. Was his attitude typical or exceptional? And what of the history and practice of surgery in the old Christendom? This might well reveal a wide spectrum of contradictory beliefs and attitudes. And I had to ask the same question about the man who consulted the astrologer after the death of his deformed son.

In sum, to learn from other faiths by the way of negative contrast can only be legitimate if one's conclusions remain tentative and open to correction in the light of wider knowledge and experience. It is very difficult to be sure that one is comparing like with like, and one needs to be guarded about generalizing from one's discoveries.

The third way in which I learn is through similarity. I find something which seems to me to be of value in Hinduism and this helps me to see something similar in Christianity.

Almost all my Hindu friends in India and in Britain keep a special room in the house which is set aside for daily worship: here are placed the images and pictures of the gods and goddesses, as well as incense sticks, little oil lamps, bells, perhaps a small vessel containing water from the Ganges, and other accoutrements of worship. Here too are kept the holy books carefully and reverently wrapped in cloth, and sometimes hung from a nail in the wall, so that they are literally in a higher and therefore more honourable place than any other books.

If the house is too small and crowded for a whole room to be set aside for this purpose, then at least a special shelf or corner in the main living room is made to serve instead.

My wife and I gradually found that the way our Hindu friends ordered their homes began to influence our own thinking. We too set aside a small room for morning and evening worship. To start with we put nothing in it except a small table with a wooden cross, our Bibles and prayer books, and a candle stick. But this was intolerably stark and bare, so we looked around for suitable pictures. Having found some and put them in the chapel we found ourselves having to ask what they were for. Were they just to look at, or were they something more than that, as the images and pictures of our Hindu friends certainly were? They performed acts of devotion before their images, and so we had to ask if this was idolatry, or if it was in any way akin to the Catholic and Orthodox use of images and pictures.[4] And then our own Evangelical background, which had said much to us about relationships, but very little about the material order, began to seem rather impoverished.

So the simple fact that our Hindu friends always set aside a special place for prayer led us to explore hitherto undiscovered areas of Christian faith and practice, to our great and continuing enrichment. Our own inherited way of being Christian began to seem somewhat arid, bookish and intellectual. This impression was deepened when I began to study the Bhagavadgita, and even more, to sit at the feet of Hindu monks and scholars as they interpreted it. This is one of the most important and popular of the Hindu sacred texts.

It is available in several good English translations and is to be found in the homes of many Hindus living in Britain. It is therefore readily accessible to the British Christian explorer.

It often speaks, as do many other of the Hindu scriptures, of the search for the divine within oneself:

> And when he draws in on every side
> His senses from their proper objects,
>   As a tortoise might its limbs,
> Firm-stablished is the wisdom of such a man.
> (Then) let him sit, curbing them all, —
> Integrated — intent on Me:
> For firm-stablished is that man's wisdom
> Whose senses are subdued.

The language of the great Christian teachers of prayer is often similar. For example Thomas à Kempis writes:

> Blessed are those who enter deeply into inner things, and daily prepare themselves to receive the secrets of heaven. Blessed are those who strive to devote themselves wholly to God, and free themselves from all the entanglements of the world. Consider these things, O my soul, and shut fast the doors against the desires of the senses, that you may hear what the Lord your God speaks within you.[5]

Here too, God is to be found within. It is not surprising therefore that Christian monks and sisters often feel an instinctive rapport with their Hindu counterparts, for they speak the same language. To say that however, is to raise the large question of how far they are talking about the same thing.

It seems at first sight that they are not, for Thomas à Kempis continues: 'And how can any creature help you, if your Creator abandon you? Set aside, therefore all else, and make yourself acceptable to your Creator, and be faithful to Him, that you may lay hold on true blessedness.'

That is language which no Hindu would use, for in Hindu thought the soul is divine by nature, a part of the divine and not created by it. But for Christians the distinction between Creator and creature is fundamental and permanent. With this is bound up our conviction that personhood is at the heart of God and that we can and must speak of his call, his purpose and his will. But this very emphasis, vital though it is, has often led us to speak of God in terms which are too anthropomorphic, cosy and familiar. On the other hand, some Christian talk about God has made him so transcendent that he has seemed altogether removed from his creation. Meeting Hindus can make us think through more clearly and more deeply what we mean when we talk of the Creator and his creation, of his transcendence and of his in-dwelling of all that he has made.

Is it possible, fourthly, to go beyond this and appropriate or 'baptize' elements of Hinduism into Christianity, elements which Christianity does not itself possess? Patently it is possible and indeed Catholics have been positively encouraged to do this since Vatican II.

The techniques of Yoga, especially its methods of breath control and bodily postures, are now widely used by Christians in Britain and elsewhere as aids to prayer.[6] Again, Hindus divide human life into four stages, each of which has its own particular disciplines and opportunities: each period of life has its own particular demands and possibilities and it is foolish to try to live at fifty in the way one did at thirty.

Some Christians are uneasy about this. They would argue that to use the techniques of Yoga, for example, is to expose oneself to the risk of being 'infected' by the philosophy on which the practice is based.

However, can we not discern a similar principle at work in the act of translating the Bible? One cannot use the words of another language without at the same time exposing oneself to the patterns of thinking on which the words are based. Every translation is a kind of 'baptism' of the language.

Here is one of those many areas where the discovery of other religions reveals the need for a deeper level of ecumenical debate and mutual understanding between Christians.

Perhaps the gulf between these two Christian outlooks is not unbridgeable. Each is appropriate for an individual or for a church, at different stages of their lives. Converts often totally reject all that they have been converted from — it is still too much of a threat for them to have anything to do with it. Yet their children can go back to the past which their parents rejected and find in it much that they want to affirm and appropriate. They are secure enough in their new faith for that return journey to be possible.

This argument can provoke British and particularly Anglican Christians to make some salutary reflections: how far is our own Christian faith and practice truly based on the gospel, and how far is that gospel simply the superficial veneer for belief and customs which are based on unexamined and therefore unredeemed presuppositions?

To talk of appropriating elements of Hinduism and of other faiths into our own is to raise that necessary question in a very sharp form. We shall have to examine it in more detail in chapter 8.

We have already moved on to the fifth stage of our ascending scale, for the boundaries between the stages are always blurred. We have to learn from Hinduism in ways which are painful, for they challenge our Christian practice.

When I was in India I was a member of a minority community. Christians numbered some three per cent of the total population of the country and were a very much smaller proportion in the area where I lived. My Hindu friends enabled me to look at the Church through their eyes. The picture they had was far from flattering. Well over ninety per cent of the Church's members across the country are drawn from outcaste groups which were and still are at the bottom of the social scale. In Hindu eyes these folk had become Christians simply in order to improve their social status, and Christianity was a foreign religion with its roots outside India.

The missionaries, of whom I was one, were perceived as the paid agents of foreign powers. 'How much money are you paid by the American government?' is a question I was often asked. We were seen as out to make converts as a means of gaining power and influence: 'You have to tell your success stories or you don't get your money from Europe and America. The whole thing is a vicious circle.'

Such criticisms cannot be brushed aside. Devotion to the success of an organization can easily and unconsciously replace devotion to God. More profoundly, the criticisms point to an inescapable fact: a church or any other community which does not seriously engage with its environment is bound to be misinterpreted to the point of caricature. When we are cast in the role of a stereotype then everything we do and say will be interpreted in its terms. But if we never dare to meet those who do the stereotyping then who is to blame for the result?

When I returned to Britain in 1978 I found the roles were reversed. It was now I who belonged to the majority community which I very soon found cast others in the role of stereotype in a way which had become only too familiar to me in India. Was it really true, I asked myself, that all Muslims were militant fundamentalists bent on taking over the country? And were all Hindus idolaters? Now that attitudes are slowly changing, and 'dialogue' is being actively encouraged by many church leaders, similar questions arise about the many new religious movements which are active in Britain today. Many of these have their roots in Hinduism. If our own impression of these groups is not formed on the basis of genuine study and encounter which has included a long time spent in listening, then are we not imprisoned in our home-made stereotypes, just as my Hindu friends in India were?

A national church has a special duty to raise these questions. Our Catholic and Free Church friends know only too well that their forebears had to do battle with ours in order to win freedom to worship and live in their own way. Will the new religious movements have to fight the same battles in the pluralist Britain of the eighties? Or can the Church of England humbly learn from its own history? It will only be able to do so if we give serious attention to the question of what it means to be one nation today. This is another issue which will occupy our attention in chapter 8.

This brings us to the sixth and final stage of our scale where the challenge is sharpest and most daunting, for it is addressed not to the way we practise our faith but to the very heart of that faith itself.

Hindus deeply resent the Christian claim that salvation is to be found *only* through Christ. This seems insufferably arrogant, the more so when it is made, as it usually is, in total ignorance of what Hindus actually believe and practise.

They will often say that all religions are the same: 'You travel to London by the motorway, we go on the train, but we all arrive at the same place.' This attitude is often, especially among members of the new movements, combined with a great admiration and sometimes even devotion to Jesus, but to a Jesus who is placed alongside Hindu gods and goddesses. Often one can see crude coloured prints of the Sacred Heart or the Good Shepherd alongside the pictures in the prayer room. Many Hindus will have read one or more of the Gospels, though very few have grappled with Paul and it is easy to understand why. The Gospels are much more accessible to the minds of those outside the Church. Paul, however, needs to be interpreted. Fewer still will have read any of the Old Testament, and those who have find it repellent. The whole notion of a chosen people, to say nothing of the holy wars in which that people engaged for much of its history, is deeply offensive to Hindus.

Further, most Hindus today are acquainted with Vedanta philosophy which asserts that the ultimate reality is beyond all the limits of 'name and form'. Devotion to images or to particular personalities such as Jesus or Muhammad, or Rama and Krishna within the Hindu tradition itself, are appropriate for people at a lower stage of spiritual development, but ultimately we must all move beyond these limits. In the words of one British Hindu of my acquaintance: 'Hinduism begins where Christianity stops.'

It is at this point that the Hindu tradition addresses its most searching challenge to Christianity, and so we must look at it in some depth.

The written sources of that challenge are to be found in some documents called the Upanishads, many of which go back to at least eight centuries before Christ. In one of these, which may be taken as typical of many though not all, a king asks a question of a great sage: 'What serves as a light for man?' The sage replies: 'The sun, your Majesty, for it is with the sun for a light that he sits, moves around, does his work and returns again.' But the king is not satisfied with this answer and so he asks another question: 'But when the sun has set, what then serves as a light for man?' The reply is 'the moon'. Still the king is not satisfied. He repeats the question twice more and the sage replies 'fire' then 'speech'. Finally the king asks: 'But when the sun has set and the moon has set and the fire has gone out and speech is silenced, what then serves as a light for man?' 'Then the Self serves as a light,' said he 'for it is with the Self as his light that he sits, moves around, does his work and returns again.' Only with this answer is the king contented.

Question and answer have led, step by step, from what is impermanent and external to man, to what is permanent and within him: the Self, which is to be found, as other Upanishads tell us, 'in the cave of the heart'. That Self is permanent and abiding. It lives on while our bodies decay and perish, and it takes on new bodies, for according to Hindu thought we are born not just once into this world, but again and again. The aim of all spiritual endeavour is to escape from this wearisome round of rebirth. To achieve this Hindus will tell us we must look within, to that cave of the heart, and there discover our true self. When we do so, we find that this is not simply our own private ego, it is one with the great divine principle or *Brahma* which underlies and pervades the universe. In the same way the drop of water is really one with the great ocean, and the spark is really one with the fire.

Our problem is not our sinfulness but our ignorance: we do not realize this unity at the heart of things. We think of ourselves as separate from other selves and we divide the world of our experience into fragments. So Hindus will often say, 'We must get beyond the sense of me and mine.'

We have to realize with our intellect that this unity is truly there, but then we have to go on to realize what we know in the depths of our experience, and that realization is beyond all words.

That means that ordinary people who stand before the images and pray are still at a lower and inadequate level of reality, at the level of separateness. They still talk of 'I *and* the god to whom I pray' of 'I *and* the world in which I live' of 'I *and* others'. Their condition is sad but not desperate, for if they don't get it right in this birth, then perhaps they will in the next one or the one after that.

And of course, among those who are still on this lower spiritual level are the Christians. For they still talk of 'God *and* I' or 'I *and* Christ'. And more often than not Christians prove they have not really arrived by the way they live, busy and active, full of good works, but essentially superficial and lacking any real depth. As a Hindu friend once put it to me after attending a church service: 'It's as if you are forever doing your exercises — standing up, sitting down, kneeling. Is there no place for stillness and silence in your religion?'

But this is not all, for many Hindus today will tell us that of course we Christians have got it all wrong, but Jesus got it all right. Did not he say: 'I and the Father are one'? He did not live on the lower level of separateness and dividedness. He knew that true unity in the heart of his own experience. It is his followers, with their dogmatism and their arrogance who have got him all wrong.

That, we may well feel, is a grievous distortion of the Christian Scriptures, and so of Jesus himself — but is it any more distorting than singing 'The heathen in his blindness bows down to wood and stone'?

There is still a very long way to go before Hindus and Christians can speak to one another with any real hope of mutual understanding. Meanwhile we are faced with the exacting but fascinating discipline of study, of listening and learning with a new humility.

What then are we to make of that Hindu experience which I have just tried to describe? Do we simply dismiss it as wrong and misguided, or worse? I for one find that I cannot do that, for I have met too many deeply impressive Hindu men and women who have claimed that this experience lies at the heart of all their living. Do I then say that their experience is the same as that which lies at the heart of my own and of all other religions, though clad in different cultural and linguistic forms? I find that suggestion far too superficial to be convincing, for the differences between religions are real: we use different language not to say the same things but to say different things. Can this experience then be somehow integrated into Christianity in the kind of way which we outlined earlier in this chapter? Some will say that it can, but before that could be possible we need to expose ourselves more deeply to its challenge than we have so far done. In other words our theology becomes unreal if it starts to move ahead of our experience. In the words of the report of the Doctrine Commission, *Believing In The Church:*

It is an urgent matter to find ways of speaking which both respect the integrity of our Muslim or Hindu neighbour and at the same time do justice to the unique significance we find in our own faith. This is an exploration which is only just beginning in our churches.[7]

This chapter has been an attempt to share what some of the fruits of that exploration could be in the context of one religious tradition. This adventure brings us back to what is always the fundamental Christian question: Who is Jesus Christ? Is he simply for some of us, who because of the accidents of history and geography happen to be Christians? Or is he in some way for all humanity? If he is indeed for all people then what practical obligation does this fact lay today upon the members of the Church of England?

To these large questions we shall be turning in our final chapter.

Notes

1. For an important development of this argument see Barbour, I., *Myths Models and Paradigms.* SCM 1981.
2. Ramsey, I. T., *Religious Language* (SCM 1957), p. 14.
3. Ecclestone, A., *Yes to God* (Darton, Longman & Todd 1975), pp. 39 – 69.
4. See chapter 4, note 1.
5. Thomas à Kempis, *The Imitation of Christ* (Penguin 1983), p. 91. Other writers in the Christian mystical tradition, such as Meister Eckhart and Jacob Boehme, can also be related to Hindu experience.
6. See, for example, J-M. Dechanet, *Christian Yoga.* Search Press 1960.
7. SPCK 1982, p. 301.

SIX

Reading the Bible with New Eyes

———

Meanwhile we are driven back to the Bible, not only because it is the basic document of our faith, but also because ministers are bound to spend a good deal of time interpreting its meaning to themselves and their congregations. Every Sunday they must delve into its ancient mysteries to come up with something which can sustain and develop the spiritual life of their congregations. When a congregation is living amid people of religion, but not the Christian religion, the pages of the Bible are apt to take on unexpected relevance. Many Christians involved in a ministry with those of other faiths have noted that familiar passages suddenly take on new meaning, and passages never before thought remarkable acquire a new importance.

This is not because the human authors of the Christian Scriptures were themselves in contact with Hindu or Buddhist believers. The whole text of the Bible was completed centuries before Muhammad and the first preachers of Islam, or the advent of Guru Nanak and the Sikh faith. In its pages there are only scattered references to the world beyond the Mediterranean basin. The Gangetic and Chinese civilizations have no place there at all. 'Tell me', wrote the great missionary to Islam, Henry Martyn, 'where in Scripture I may find India?' There is in fact a fleeting trace of it. Jesus, intriguingly, is recorded as having been taken down from the cross and wrapped in a *sindōn* (Mark 15.46; Matt. 27.59; Luke 23.53). This word has traditionally been translated as 'a linen sheet', but it should almost certainly be understood as a length of cotton cloth imported from Sindh, in India (now Pakistan), whence its name (cf. also Mark 14. 51 — 52). But the very unexpectedness — for us, the delight — of such a reference betrays how rare it is in our Scriptures. Our theology of other faiths, our Christian theology of religion, has to take the Bible as what Kenneth Cragg has called its 'field of precedents', rather than as a handbook of explicit judgements and directions. It is the Spirit who must guide us, and be the reader of the Scriptures in us.

As he does so, many passages will come to life in a new way, reflecting our new experiences with those of other faiths. The Old Testament in particular has taken on a new vitality in our minds, and we have felt engaged in a new way by the sagas of the patriarchs of Genesis, and by the concerns revealed in the legal material of the Pentateuch — material actually printed in small type in some editions of the Bible, on the assumption that it is of less interest or value than the rest. So much of characteristic religious behaviour all over the world is reflected here. Abraham and Jacob travel through the land marking those places where they experience God's presence with special shrines. Household images, fertility symbols, the ancient deception and guile of the Middle East permeate the story of Jacob and his sons. The great story of God's rescue in Exodus is punctuated with shamanistic tricks, and merges into a series of long treatises concerned with the proper form of sacrifice, and the correct ways to maintain purity and avoid ritual pollution. In so many ways the people of the biblical records were at one with people of religion of almost all times and places. Holy places, holy words and books, holy furniture and personnel, pilgrimage, fasting, festival and prayer — all these things are common to all religious traditions, and when you live within sight of the gurdwara and the mosque the Bible's words about them become more pointed. The Bible, moreover, is no longer the province of the theologian alone. A number of anthropologists have been sufficiently attracted by the wealth of material in the Old Testament to draw illuminating parallels between some of its scenes and the records of their own field work. Mary Douglas's classic study on the 'Abominations of Leviticus'[1] explores the idea of pollution and the dietary law that follows from it in a way that throws light on Judaism, Hinduism and other cultures all over the world, including our own.

In the work of anthropologists one thing becomes very plain: the assumptions we bring to our reading of the Bible profoundly affect the message we think we take from it. If, like Gandhi and many Hindus, we think that no particular importance should be attached to any historical events, then like him we may conclude that it would not matter if it could be proved that Jesus of Nazareth never actually existed, for the story of his life would still be inspiring. If, however, like many Muslims we regard the Christian Scriptures as valuable but not in their present form totally reliable, we may conclude with them that the end of Jesus's life on earth, like its beginning, is shrouded in mystery and that its real importance lies in the teaching which he brought, in common with all the prophets, from God.

These are examples of a general principle that becomes more significant as the reader of the Bible moves out of his own native culture and begins to share the understandings and assumptions of the rest of the world. What do I bring to the Bible? Certainly not a mind which is a *tabula rasa*. I bring all my own experience, and my own prejudices, examined and unexamined, regretted and unregretted, and all the cultural baggage of the way that I and my people live. I can do no other. There is a certain naivety which comes over many people when they speak about the teaching of the Bible, as though its message must be instantly obvious and agreed among all right-thinking people as soon as sufficient attention is paid to it. We speak in our creeds of the Spirit 'who spake through the prophets'. But if the Spirit is the true author of the Scriptures, is he not also the true reader of them? Too often we forget that the 'man who is unspiritual refuses what belongs to the Spirit of God; it is folly to him; he cannot grasp it, because it needs to be judged in the light of the Spirit' (1 Cor. 2.14). And the Spirit is not given just to individuals but to people who live in communities, and who in many ways think and believe as those communities make possible.[2]

One of the most startling of many 'misreadings' of the New Testament is recounted in Chaim Potok's novel *In the Beginning* when a twelve-year-old Jewish boy, brought up in the strictest New York Orthodoxy, gets hold of a copy of the New Testament for the first time in his life, and looks through it, hunting feverishly for the passages which tell Christians to hate Jews.[3] If of course you are convinced such passages are there, because that is what your own people have told you, you will find them, notably in the fourth Gospel and parts of

Matthew. This is one of the many occasions when we dare not forget the subsequent history of the Church when we read the Bible, in case we fail to notice how its message has at times been hideously distorted. We cannot simply jump back to the first century as if nothing had intervened. The current storm-centre of New Testament study is whether some of the New Testament writers were genuinely anti-Judaic, or whether they unknowingly offered ammunition to subsequent Christians who did hate Jews.[4]

What then, does the Spirit say to the person who reads his Bible with some background knowledge and experience of meeting with people of other faiths? The scale of God's intention, concern and activity is enormously enlarged in our minds as we read anew. Commentators on the Gospels have often noted that Mark, the earliest of the four, begins the story of Jesus with John the Baptist in the wilderness, and a glance back to Isaiah's prophecy. Matthew begins with a genealogy which starts with Abraham. Luke begins his version of the genealogy with Adam, while John takes us back to the beginning of all things. Clearly the evangelists only gradually perceived the appropriate scale on which Jesus's life needed to be recounted. Our own experience is bound to echo this, and we should expect the Spirit to enlarge our understanding and 'guide us into all the truth' (John 16.13). He does so in showing us how from the beginning God's concern was for the whole world, in all its bewildering variety. We are accustomed to quoting, with the appropriate emphasis, 'God so loved the *world.* . . .' not just the Church, but it is when we turn back to the early pages of Genesis, searching for God's purposes with the nations of the world, that we realize how self-centred we have been, and how the whole human race is God's concern. Not only is creation, as in few other holy books, placed at the forefront and outset of the whole text, but the nations are listed in symbolic form in Genesis 10, and even when the focus of attention narrows to the descendants of Shem, and then of Abraham, then of Isaac, then of Jacob, the collateral descendants are never entirely forgotten, and genealogical reminders of them appear consistently to punctuate the text. These little-noted passages may never be read in church, and would clearly not feature in any scheme of reading the Bible drawn up for a new believer, but the fact that they are there is still of importance. Comedians have made fun of 'all that begetting', but we need to be reminded that the Bible's concentration on one small group of tribes in the Middle East is a highly selective reading of world history, and that the biblical authors were well aware of the fact. The long-forgotten names preserve a perspective of God's care for the world, and for the whole of humanity which confirms our own new experience. Here we realize anew that God's choice of some is for the sake of all the rest. If the biblical record appears to abandon interest in those outside the narrow compass of Palestine, it is only so that his fundamental purposes for all may be accomplished.

This is a vital point to grasp in the face of those who accuse Christians of insularity and narrow-mindedness. As we have seen, Hindus tend to criticize the whole Christian tradition for its exclusiveness, and much discussion has focused on the person of Christ and the question of a unique salvation through him. This is sometimes referred to as the 'scandal of particularity'. But it is important to be clear that the criticism of Hindus, and of those in the West like John Hick who sympathize with them, implicitly involves the whole biblical record. For the 'scandal of particularity' did not begin with Jesus, but goes back to Genesis 12, with Abraham. As the biblical writers see it, God chose to make his reckoning with the human race through one particular people. The experience of being God's covenant people, so alien a concept to some minds, involves the possibility both of relationship with God and of apostasy from him. For those outside the covenant neither is strictly possible, except through relationship with the Jews.

What kind of relationship was envisaged, then, between the Jews themselves and those aliens who, for one reason or another, took up residence among them and submitted to the rule of the covenant people? The resident alien, whether exile or migrant or refugeee, has normally had a hard time in human history. Landless, sometimes language-less, and often resource-less, he has few ways of helping himself other than by long hours of menial work, and is often the object of both contempt and suspicion. Yet such 'sojourners' or 'strangers' were accorded distinct rights in Jewish law. The memory of the wanderings of the patriarchs, and particularly the years of slavery in Egypt were to act as a spur for generous treatment of the stranger. 'If a stranger lives with you in your land, do not molest him. You must count him as one of your own countrymen and love him as yourself — for you were once strangers yourselves in Egypt. I am the LORD your God' (Lev. 19.33.) — 'It is God who sees justice done for the orphan and the widow, who loves the stranger and gives him food and clothing. Love the stranger then, for you were strangers in the land of Egypt' (Deut. 10.18, 19). In this way the stranger is a test case, like the widow and the orphan, of the believer's sincerity in his faith, and his obedience and love of God (cf. Jas. 1.27). But more than that, the stranger actually becomes a permanent reminder to the Jews of their own past, and of God's rescue of them from wretchedness in a foreign land. They are called to become rescuers in their turn, following God's example of redemption. For they, like all God's human creation, were to be like him (Gen. 1.27). The stranger embodied in himself a kind of parable of God's care for all people, especially those undergoing hardship and suffering.

All this and more lies behind the story Jesus told which we know as the parable of the Good Samaritan. In the Law the stranger was the one who took advantage of the stalks of corn which had been overlooked, or the olives left on the tree after it had been beaten to bring them down. He was the sharer in the feast, but remained marginal, passed over. His potential as a living reminder of God's goodness was often ignored. So Jesus deliberately took one of the most problematic communities known to the Jews of his day, and made a member of it the hero in a story of rescue and liberation. When neither Levite nor priest would help, the stranger came to the rescue. From being one for whom Jews should care because they also knew what it was to be aliens, the stranger becomes one who brings care to the Jew himself. The Jew in the story received from the hands of a heretical stranger, hardly to be counted as a believer, the indispensable care without which he would have died. Here is an immensely powerful witness to the fundamental concern of God for all people, whatever their race or creed or culture, and to the mutual concern and care which they should have in consequence for each other. They are to be mutually dependent. When that law of God is flouted, and his demand for mutual care ignored, judgement is passed on the priest and the Levite who turn aside from the task of rescue. It is not difficult to see the application to our own society, especially in its dealings with struggling minorities.

Moreover Jesus himself comes as a stranger in the Gospels. 'He came to his own home, and his own people received him not' (John 1.11). ' "Is not this, the carpenter, the son of Mary . . . . And are not his sisters here with us?" So they fell foul of him' (Mark 6.3). At the crisis of his life even Peter treated him as a stranger and denied he knew him. Yet Jesus said to them 'I was a stranger and you welcomed me. . . as you did it to one of the least of these my brethren, you did it to me.' (Matt. 25.35, 40). So the stranger becomes a mystery who carries in his own person the reminder and the sign of the gospel. Christians themselves are strangers, 'the unknown men whom all men know' (2 Cor. 6.9), 'aliens in a foreign land' (1 Pet. 2.11). Yet Christians have managed to manipulate their vocation to 'strangerhood' into domesticity. In 1 Peter 1.17 (' . . . throughout the time of your exile' — RSV) the word variously translated 'on earth' (NEB), 'living away from home' (JB), 'as strangers' (NIV), is *paroikia,* the abstract noun from one of the standard Greek words for 'stranger'. In the early Church the same word meant, by extension, the community of such strangers, and hence an ecclesiastical unit. From there it developed, via Latin and French, into the familiar 'parish', and 'parochial'.

It is true of course, that this account of the biblical theme of the 'stranger' cannot in any case be made to yield straightforward policies for a plural society as we know it today. We would regard freedom of worship as basic to a modern democratic society, yet the resident alien, the *ger* of Jewish law had no such freedom. He had to keep the Sabbath (Exod. 20.10; 23.12), and was expected to join in the great festivals (Deut. 16.10 ff). He was not permitted to worship any god except the Lord of Israel, even though he only shared in the Passover if he were circumcised (Exod. 12.48).

Just as the ancient biblical law cannot easily be turned into modern legislation, so the unwary preacher has to read his Bible very carefully to avoid being caught up in racist attitudes. There is no doubt that the Bible can be used to support apartheid and other forms of racial discrimination. A casual reading of Joshua 23, for example, as it appears in the Anglican ASB lectionary (Morning Prayer for Pentecost 19, year 2), could unleash a fine sermon for the National Front: 'You must not associate with the peoples that are left among you: you must not call upon their gods by name . . . For your sake the Lord has driven out great and mighty nations . . . if you do turn away and attach yourselves to the people that still remain among you, and intermarry with them and associate with them and they with you, then be sure . . . they will be snares to entrap you.' Similarly Nehemiah 13 (admittedly a weekday rather than a Sunday reading) gives a graphic account of Nehemiah's attempts to combat intermarriage and to preserve Jewish religious and racial purity. How do we understand such passages today? If we are not careful they may simply be an embarrassment to us, and our awkwardness about them may make us helpless against the person who comes to the Bible to justify his racism.

Perhaps the first thing is to see how such stories would appear to Asians. It is likely that Muslims, Hindus and Sikhs would have no difficulty in identifying with the sentiments of Joshua and Nehemiah in relation to this country. For them indeed the danger is compromise, and assimilation into the majority culture. They do indeed see their children growing up, as Nehemiah complained was happening to Jewish children, unable to speak the language of their parents and to understand the sacred ceremonies conducted in that language. It is bad enough for white Christian parents to watch their own children drift away from the faith of their fathers and become indistinguishable from the secular majority, apart perhaps from a certain wistful respect for religion. At least such parents remain united to their children in many other areas of life. But Asian parents risk seeing their children entering a world they themselves know nothing of, and becoming totally divorced from the lives and values of their families. When they consider the long years of hardship and exile from all that is most familiar and cherished, they must wonder whether it has all been worth it, or whether they have not made a tragic mistake. In such circumstances, and watching perhaps the experience of some other families, it would be surprising if the reaction were not a fierce determination to prevent it from happening. Already teachers of Urdu and Bengali testify that the children they teach, sons and daughters of native speakers, understand only the merest colloquialisms in those languages. Any prolonged discussion is beyond them, and to sustain it they drop into English, the language of their education.

For all our sympathy, however, we cannot read Nehemiah that way for ourselves. How do we read him then? Here, it seems, is a call primarily to integrity of life, of wholehearted loyalty to the Lord which is determined to put him first. 'Set your mind on God's kingdom and his justice before everything else, and all the rest will come to you as well' (Matt. 6.33). We will not, however, go around beating our fellow Christians and tearing out their hair (Neh. 13.25), for we can share Nehemiah's fundamental concern without adopting his prescription. Indeed we may not, for we are heirs to Jesus as well as Nehemiah, and in the light of his coming all racial pride is dissolved and all anxiety for our own communal well-being is lost in the overwhelming vitality of the wholeness he gives. For us biological growth is not the only possibility. The message of the resurrection brings in new members and we are enabled to be free from ethnocentricity. But in any case our problem is the opposite of that faced by Hindus, Muslims and Sikhs. They face the loss of identity by absorption into the majority. We, members racially of the majority, face an impoverishment of identity by our refusal to engage with the new neighbours whom the Lord has given us. If we refuse to learn anything new from them, the result is that we become less able and willing to learn anything new, and therefore to grow as people and as disciples.

The Christian Scriptures are entirely realistic about our need to be affirmed by God and equally about the necessity to protect the people of God from contaminating influences. In all the diatribes against idolatry, even the great satirical attack of Isaiah 44, it is the Israelites who are addressed, and the Israelites who are warned to be faithful to the Lord and not to fall into the errors of the surrounding nations. In the New Testament this emphasis is never wholly abandoned, but a new note is heard, the theme of the 'righteous Gentile'.[5] Among many incidents in the Gospels perhaps the most striking is the healing of the ten lepers, in which the only one to return to give thanks to God was a Samaritan (Luke 17. 18 – 19). Jesus says: 'Could none be found to come back and give praise to God except this *allogenes* (foreigner)?' The point here is that this word is otherwise known only from the Septuagint and from the inscription in the Temple at Jerusalem which prevented non-Jews (*allogenes*) from going further into the Temple on pain of death. Yet Jesus says to this disqualified non-person: 'Your faith has saved (or cured) you.'

Again and again, especially in Luke, we see that the people who ought to have known, the people most qualified to recognize and accept God's Messiah, are the very ones who reject and attempt to crush him. It is the outsiders, in contrast, Samaritans, Roman soldiers, the Syro-Phoenician woman, who have faith and respond. Judgement, we are reminded, begins at the household of God (1 Pet. 4.17). In a critically important passage for our day, Paul in Romans 9 – 11 reminds his Gentile readers that since they have benefited from Jewish inability to accept the gospel, it is inappropriate for them to feel superior to Jews. God's intention will not finally be frustrated. Meanwhile there are others who will hear and respond.

There is a special connection between the New Testament passages concerning the Samaritans and modern attitudes towards Muslims. Jews and Samaritans had what in some cultures are called 'avoidance relations'. They were sufficiently close, in geographical and theological terms, to threaten each other. Sharing some of the same scriptures and much of the same history, they were both very close and miles apart. In the years before the times of Jesus there had been a number of incidents which set the two communities at loggerheads. So the prominence which Jesus gives to Samaritans in his parables and in his personal encounters is remarkable. Part of our Christian problem with Islam is that historically it postdates Christianity and contains a critique of Christian faith in its foundation document, the Qur'an. In one sense Islam is a response to historic Christianity (but not necessarily to the true Christian gospel). This makes it both difficult and urgent to find biblical clues which can help us assess Islam. The Samaritans as they appear in the pages of the New

Testament are one such clue. John 4 repays much study here, for Jesus makes it clear that salvation comes from the Jews (v. 22), and yet he refuses to accept the Jewish case in the quarrel between Jews and Samaritans. That particular argument centred on the worship acceptable to God, whether it was to be offered on Mount Gerizim or in Jerusalem. Jesus said neither, but that true worship would be offered to the Father in spirit and in truth.

Arguments between Christians and Muslims have often centred in a similar way upon modes of worship, and whether God listened to the prayers of Muslims or Christians. Christians have often claimed that prayer is only valid through Jesus, while for Muslims that very condition is enough to invalidate prayer otherwise acceptable. Jesus's key remark to the woman was that 'You Samaritans worship without knowing what you worship, while we worship what we know.' Innumerable converts to Christianity from Islam have said that the God they worshipped in Islam without knowing him they now worship as Christians having seen and recognized him in Jesus.

There is of course no simple correspondence between the situation of New Testament times and our own. Nevertheless consistent preaching of this message should produce a Christian people who are not unduly impressed by their own faithfulness or deluded into supposing that it was for some special quality of their own that God sought them out in Christ. If people with the advantages in faith of first-century Israelites could go astray, how much more conceivable is it that we also might blunder. The history of the Church at least in the West does not give much cause for complacency. In regard to other believers in their neighbourhood Christians may well conclude that God has not left himself without witness (Acts 14.17), and that, as in the past, he is inclined to reveal his word through unlikely messengers, and to produce faith in unexpected places.

If a single book in the Bible is needed as reminder of that, it is perhaps the book of Job. Job's identity is uncertain, though he was probably an Edomite or a Transjordanian sheikh. The only recognizable names in the book are Edomite. Unless he was altogether a fiction we can be sure that he was not an Israelite, for he nowhere refers to Israelite history, cult or law, and therefore despite some commentaries can hardly be said to have believed in the God of Israel. Here we have a text which speaks with tremendous power of suffering and faith — universal themes — and yet we have almost no idea of its provenance. The proverbial wisdom of Edom may be a clue. Job, anyway, becomes proverbial himself for righteousness (Ezek. 14.14, 20), and sums up a long line of godly men and women who lacked the advantage of being Israelites: Jethro, Rahab, Ruth and Naaman.

To say all this, and indeed to underline it in one's preaching, is not to settle for any kind of theological relativism. The Christological question, which is at heart a question about God as much as about Jesus, remains. The question about salvation also remains, and we shall be returning to both of them in our last chapter.

Notes

1. Douglas, M., *Purity and Danger. An Analysis of Concepts of Pollution and Taboo* (Routledge & Kegan Paul 1966), pp. 41—57.
2. See The Doctrine Commission of the Church of England: *Believing in the Church. The Corporate Nature of Faith.* SPCK 1981.
3. Potok, Chaim, *In the Beginning* (Penguin edn, 1976), p. 316 f.
4. See Leech, K., ed. *Theology and Racism — 1: The Bible, Racism and Anti-Semitism.* Church of England Board for Social Responsibility 1985.
5. This Jewish term reminds us, of course, that the roots of Jesus's teaching and attitude to non-Jews is found in such passages as Isaiah 56. 3—8.

SEVEN

The Church School and Other Ministries

So far we have said nothing about a subject that looms large in the minds of some clergy—the educational responsibilities which the Church of England took on in the last century and which stay with us in the form of the voluntary aided church school (less commonly the voluntary controlled school, with its smaller degree of church involvement). We feel, however, that this concern needs to be considered alongside others which also belong to the institutional character of the Church's impact on society, rather than to its internal life. There are situations—a surprising number of them—in which the history and significance of the Church of England in particular, and to a lesser extent other churches, has brought about a certain recognition of the local clergyman as a necessary presence, or at least an accepted element in a number of statutory bodies. Everyone is familiar with the fact that there are hospital chaplains, prison chaplains, student chaplains. There are also, increasingly, Christians working part- or full-time in local radio stations with a particular concern for religious broadcasting, and some of these people are Anglican clergy.

Often this kind of work is fitted in to an already crowded life, with little time to reflect on the issues that such involvement raises. For the most part the clergyman paying a regular, but brief visit to an old people's home or a local factory where he has been made welcome, does not have time to ask himself how he might measure the difference his visit makes, or in what sense his presence, brief as it is, contributes to a more humane and even godly state of affairs. He is glad enough to be welcome, perhaps glad to have contacts outside the regular congregation, glad enough, no doubt, to be a visible reminder of the significance of faith in a world which seems very short of it. But when the places he visits, or his formal responsibilities, include people of other faiths, the issue immediately surfaces as to *which* faith is significant, and if Christianity, why not Islam; if the Christian priest comes, why not the Hindu, or the imam; if this religious observance why not that? These issues are there, of course, even without the clergyman's being present. In one school the concession that Muslim girls might wear their traditional baggy trousers brought forward the demand that white English girls should be allowed to wear *their* traditional leg-coverings, i.e. jeans. But there is no doubt that the institutional involvement of the Church in any secular concern, by means of the clergyman, does complicate matters.

At present, except in the educational field, these are potential issues rather than actual disputes, questions just below the surface which we shall try to tackle at their root in our final chapter. One reason for this is the absence, as yet, of any real acceptance of a *pastoral* role by the imam, priest or even rabbi. The latter is indeed often pressed by his 'congregants' (to use the significantly different Jewish term) to behave more like a Christian minister, but his basic training and understanding of his role is that of a learned man, a person who can be trusted to interpret the religious law correctly and to lead worship in a fitting and proper way. Similarly with the imam. There has, it is true, been a development in some *yeshivas* (Jewish seminaries) towards training potential rabbis in the skills of counselling, in particular. But essentially these religious leaders are holy men — the seeker goes to the holy man (or more rarely, woman); the holy man does not search out the seeker.

There is in consequence not the demand that there might be for Muslim and Sikh and other religious leaders to be allowed the same rights of access to hospital, school, prison and radio station as the Christian clergy. Of course some patients and prisoners may ask if they can see a leader of their own faith, but their concern is more likely to be that they should be able to observe their own dietary rules or have opportunity to pray in what to them is the proper manner. Frequently the full-time hospital and prison chaplains have taken the initiative in trying to secure these facilities for those of other faiths under their care. One is then compelled to ask 'What is actually happening here?' At one level the Christian minister is simply ensuring that the facilities extended through him and by tradition are not denied to those whose traditions and language are different. If religious freedom, like other freedoms, is indivisible, then a refusal to offer such practical help to those of other faiths might eventually lead to a situation where Christians are also deprived. Such a step is perhaps more important in that the prevailing secularity of our culture rarely acknowledges religious faith to be of more than minor importance, a private aberration. The chaplain's assistance is then seen as a blow not merely for community relations and intercultural tolerance and understanding, but obliquely for the faith itself.

However, another interpretation is possible. What, after all, is the relation between 'faith' and 'the faith', as employed in the argument above? Is there a widespread common experience which we call 'faith', which takes different forms in different cultures, but which is easily recognizable despite the very varied dogmas and customs which cluster around it, some better, some poorer expressions of this experience, but all in their own way valid? This, so it seems, is essentially what is believed by many millions of our own contemporaries, and expressed with great sophistication and learning by such people as Wilfred Cantwell Smith.[1] The difficulty appears to be to give any satisfactory content to what, or whom, it is that one has faith in. How do we know that it is essentially the same faith when it is expressed so differently, when the formulations of one school are totally rejected by another, and religion itself seems to play so drastically different a role in society from, for example, Thailand or Iran to Poland or Uganda? One need not go all the way into a cast-iron exclusive position where only we (or rather I) are endowed with any grasp of the truth, to see that the simple equation of 'faith' and 'the faith' (or more often the dropping of the latter) will not do.

Yet, to return to our chaplain, will it not appear that this is the plain implication of his actions? Many at least will assume that his cause and that of his Muslim colleague are identical, unless they are people who know sufficient about both faiths to realize the incompatibility that adherents of both would acknowledge. It seems to us, however, that this is a risk worth taking for the sake of the genuine common ground which exists between Christianity and Islam, and for the sake of the human rights that Muslims and other people of religion should be freely granted. After all, the freedom to worship as one's conscience directs was achieved at the cost of much blood in this country, and it could easily be lost again. It was, we should remember, sharply resisted by the Church of England. That freedom includes unrestricted access to the personnel and facilities which, for many, are essential to worship. The hospital chaplain may serve here as the model for a range of Christian clergy serving within some local or national institution who are prepared to accept that the presence of faiths other than Christianity imposes obligations of assistance on them. It must be admitted, however, that we have hardly begun to see the fuller implications or development of this, and that the participation of religious leaders of other faiths in national affairs — e.g. leading prayers each day at the opening of the business of Parliament — is likely to be fraught with controversy.

At present, however, the controversy is in a different area, and centres not on the articulate demands of adults for themselves, but on the delicate assessment of the needs of their children. It is in education that the debate is in full swing, and on a multitude of topics. First, however, it would be well to note that the Church has from the beginning had two motives in its involvement in education. For some the prime issue was the access of children of all social classes and regions to a soundly-based and practically useful education. The State had determined on universal primary education, but had not the means to provide it. The Church was able, in some areas massively, to assist. For others, however, it was the quality of Christian nurture which the Church could provide, moulding the believers of the next generation, which mattered. Such motivation lay behind Free Church and Roman Catholic schools in particular, but was not absent from the Church of England schools. For many, as today, the two concerns existed side by side without apparent conflict. Once, however, the traditional locality served by a church school received large numbers of children of other faiths, the conflict was bound to emerge. (It should be noted here that children of Afro-Caribbean origin, who were here from the mid-50's, did not pose this problem, because most of their parents had some connection, however nominal, with the churches of the West Indies, and many were fervent believers. The problem there was blatant racial prejudice, but it was a racial and not a religious problem.)

What does the church school do about its admission procedures when its traditional locality has become, in part at least, Muslim and Hindu and Sikh rather than (at least nominally) Christian? It may carry on, if it can, with a school population recruited with some kind of Christian credential. If this is even superficially successful it will create a school which is white, with some West Indian children, depending on the character of the local population and the reputation of the school. In the same area, for the same reasons, there will be one or more state schools which are predominantly Asian. Both types of school will be ghetto schools, unrepresentative of the area they serve, with the additional problem that the Asian-dominated schools will be avoided by white parents, many of whom will be tempted to feign 'Christian' credentials in order to secure admission for their children into the church school. Christianity and culture thereby become hopelessly confused, and the church school is open to serious charges of racism, despite its West Indian pupils. This is actually happening in some parts of the country.

In practice few Church of England schools appear to have followed this policy, though Roman Catholic schools, with their different history of minority status, now sometimes find themselves in that unenviable position. Other church schools have either allowed unrestricted entry to children of other faiths, or established a set quota of such children, who thus become a permanent, though minority part of the school. Admission policy is only, however, the beginning of a series of new and sometimes controversial decisions which have to be taken. Should the school's Board of Governors include one or more members of the minority faith now represented in the school—perhaps a parent or a leader of the local Muslim or Sikh community? If it does so, what becomes of its claim to be a Christian school? And how can it ensure that the primary motivating force in the life of the school is a Christian one?

These may seem somewhat abstract and rarified questions to some, though they have been the subject of acute and sustained discussion in similar cases abroad, where a school or hospital founded by missionaries has to face the decision of employing Hindu or Muslim teachers or medical staff, or of accepting on the central board of management people who do not adhere to the faith of the founders. At what point does a Christian institution cease to be such? In England the Church has long accepted the principle of partnership with the State in education. Can this be extended, in appropriate circumstances, to communities of another faith, and if so, under what circumstances? Education, with its 'hidden curriculum' of philosophical and ideological presuppositions, obviously poses a more acute problem than the practice of medicine or social welfare, where the interpretation of world events and ideas is not directly involved. On the other hand is there not some 'common ground', as already mentioned, on which religious people can unite to resist the prevailing secularism?

This issue arises in Britain primarily with Muslims, since they are the largest minority faith community, with articulate and well-organized spokesmen. Moreover Christianity undeniably has more theological ground in common with Islam than with any other faith except Judaism. It happens also that Asian Muslims, not having had the Jewish exposure to the last three hundred years of European history, and not being therefore co-heirs of the Enlightenment, are much more critical of the assumptions of modernity, and much less inclined to take for granted our western attitudes to education. One way of expressing educational aims commonly agreed in Britain would be in the aphorism: 'I train a dog to live with me: I train a child to live without me'. Muslims would find such emphasis on the capacity for independent thought and action deeply destructive of the unity of the family and the whole structure of traditional culture. Do we not need to hear such radical criticism, and does not religious faith have a particular concern for a creative continuity with the past? How else can we know who we are, if we do not respond to a set of shared memories? If, as we have argued elsewhere in this book, many in our society need a 'healing of memories', our children too need to be initiated into shared understandings, and it is at least possible that in this process people of other faiths can be creative partners, recalling us to things we might otherwise neglect.

In encountering the traditional culture of the people of India and Pakistan we have often felt we were confronting our own past. Consider the phrases of the 1662 Catechism, and how they apply still to the hierarchical societies of South Asia and elsewhere:

> My duty is to . . . love, honour, and succour my father and mother; to submit myself to all my governors, teachers, spiritual pastors and masters; to order myself lowly and reverently to all my betters . . . and to do my duty in that state of life unto which it shall please God to call me.

In a book like Peter Laslett's *The World We Have Lost*[2], about Stuart England, we can feel the social force of that inculcated deference, with its powerful religious sanction, which we still meet in South Asian, and some West Indian families today. How different is the modern ethic, here expressed by a leading Tory politician: 'The inescapable duty is to take personal responsibility for one's own thought and action.'

If we were to set down, in an admitted caricature, the main features of Modern, as compared with Traditional values, it might look like this: *Traditional* — unquestioning respect and obedience to others, especially the elders of one's own family; a positive valuation of dependence; concern for the reputation of the family (understood of course as the extended family); educational and career advance viewed as a family asset; segregated socializing; arranged marriages. Contrasting *Modern* values would be[3] — respect has to be earned, but is more readily given to the peer group and to media stars; a high valuation on independence and learning from one's own experience; a person's reputation his or her own achievement and largely unaffected by other members of the family; educational and career advancement to develop individual potential which the family should not hinder; mixed socializing and the selection of a life partner proceeding through trial and error. Viewed in this way the contrasts are sharp and the mutual criticisms predictable. The Traditionals find that the Modern emphasis on self-discovery in education and ethics seems to put a premium on ignorance and anarchy.

The slighting of elders and family cohesiveness looks like wanton and foolish impudence. The concern for personal self-fulfilment is a selfish luxury. The trial and error method of relating to the opposite sex produces principally error, and painful, damaging and ungodly error at that. The Moderns see the Traditional ways as stultifying and hypocritical, blocking all possibility of genuine self-awareness and therefore of genuine encounter with others. The demand for outward respect produces deviousness and underhand solutions to problems which need plain speaking. The family and its extended community become a prison, or at best a means by which the needs and obligations of the larger community are side-stepped.

All these values and counter-values are inevitably at stake in the education of children, and the surprising thing is perhaps not that Muslims and some others have wanted to establish their own schools, but that they have so often been content to make use of church schools. The reason often given for this is that God is felt to be taken seriously in a church school, and the whole of education conducted under a kind of religious umbrella. This is no doubt valid as far as it goes, but it needs to be recognized that for many people 'God' may serve as an umbrella term to include the Traditional values listed above. For this reason the attitudes of other faith parents to church schools have often been deeply ambivalent. On the one hand they are seen as a definite improvement on state schools, with their explicit religious commitment and a seriousness about the things of faith. On the other hand parents from the Muslim community in particular may well be nervous of too overt a Christian emphasis, and also critical that Modern values still find too congenial a home in the church school. For this complex of reasons they may press for Muslim children to be withdrawn from school assembly, and arrangements made for a local imam to give classes of Muslim children special instruction in their faith.

How is the local Anglican vicar, who may find himself Chairman of the Board of Governors of a church school, to respond to such a situation? In practice responses have ranged from a total refusal to allow any withdrawal or any teaching about other faiths, on the grounds that parents agree from the outset that their children are to be part of a church school; to the open invitation and welcome to the imam to conduct Muslim worship regularly at the normal times of school assembly. These responses will of course be determined by the theological understanding (or misunderstanding) of the Governors about other faiths, and probably about Islam in particular, and they are likely to look to the vicar, as Chairman, for that. His lead will depend very much on his personal acquaintance with people of other faiths, and his knowledge of the cultures shaped by those faiths, as well as on his formal theological 'position'.

Our own advice on the question of school assembly would depend to some extent on the composition of the school. If, as in a few church schools, there is actually a majority of children of other faiths (one or two have *only* Muslim pupils), it is obviously quite impossible to conduct worship as if the children were even nominally Christian. One might read from the Bible, both Old and New Testaments, and use the parables of Jesus in particular, but to sing hymns in praise of Jesus would seem to be an exploitation of the children, and thus, in the end, counter-productive. Nothing can be lost, and a great deal gained, by a thorough and consistent respect for the integrity of all concerned. Indeed it is difficult to see how worship can be carried out in any meaningful way without it. Where theological considerations prevent, for example, the use of the formula 'through Jesus Christ our Lord' there may be ways of explaining the difficulty which actually enhance the understanding of the children and their respect for religious belief, and for Christian forbearance in particular. At other times it may be right to invite Muslim children to engage in their own form of worship in the presence of the rest of the school, who are thereby enabled to share, as reverent observers, something of great importance to the Muslim community. At other times it may be right to conduct a Christian Eucharist in the same way. It seems to us that in the kind of school community we are envisaging here, what binds the children together is not common belief but a common respect for religious belief, and a concern to see it expressed and lived out with integrity. This would not indeed be sufficient to sustain a church, but here we are dealing with the school and not with the church in another form. The school too, must be allowed its own integrity. Many devout Religious Education teachers recognize this, even in all-white schools, by carefully separating their professional task of teaching the RE syllabus, which happens in the classroom where all must attend, from an evangelistic concern for their pupils.

In a similar way it seems to us that in no way can the Christian faith become 'compulsory' in a church school, even if parents appear to sign away their rights to anything else by entering their child in such a school. If children are to respond to the Christian faith in freedom, no kind of manipulation can be allowed. On the other hand the presentation of the Christian faith cannot be merely 'objective', as it may be in the state school, as dispassionate a description of the human history and present realities as can be managed. In a church school Christianity must be more than described; it must be in some sense *pre*scribed. To put it in the curious jargon of the sociologists, the church school should be a 'structure of plausibility' for the Christian gospel, a place where the gospel becomes in course of time compelling, though never compulsory, a corporate experience where those outside the church community may begin to think that 'perhaps it may really be so'.

Some will find this too tentative a hope, and too slender an experience for their own more boisterous faith and ambitions. We would remind them of the cost of true evangelism and the intense pain of many a Christian conversion to the Muslim or Hindu family in which it has taken place. Others may find our 'prescription' too much like a presumption that all truth belongs to us and that we have the right to propagate it at will. To them we have to say that everyone expects that there should be some difference between a church school and a state one, and that for reasons explained earlier that difference cannot be simply to do with 'faith', unqualified. For faith is never found unqualified, and to be faithful the Christian has to commend Christ, in his words, his silences and his daily being.

One way of elaborating the kind of school community we envisage is to take the four principles of dialogue outlined in the publications of the British Council of Churches[4], and see how they might apply to the situation of the church school which has a number of pupils of other faiths in it. The first principle says that: *Dialogue begins when people meet each other.* Here is an obvious but urgently necessary reminder, for people of sincere faith and none are equally ready to argue about the characteristics of impersonal systems of belief like Hinduism, Buddhism or Christianity. But we do not ordinarily meet Hinduism or Islam; we meet Hindus and Muslims, and the truth about the cultures they represent is far better served if we are in personal touch with them. It is true that twelve-year old Khalid may not be very well informed about his own faith, but the fact that he is there as a Muslim in the classroom ought to transform the teacher's treatment of Muhammad, the Crusades, and the Third World. Equally important is the grasp of different cultures, and the convictions that inform them. If Joshi joins the vegetarian queue at lunchtime his English friends have the opportunity to learn more about what is involved in eating meat than they might have done otherwise. Similarly with the Muslim prescriptions on modesty in dress, and against mixed bathing.

The second principle is really an extension of the first: *Dialogue depends upon mutual understanding and mutual trust.* The church school is a place where that rare flower may grow. If it is to do so it will need a very careful nurturing in the RE classroom in particular, but those teaching History and English literature will also have to beware of the stereotypes that creep unobserved into our common speech and betray our prejudices. The kind of integrity we have been advocating is an essential ingredient of 'mutual understanding and mutual trust'.

The fruits of all this will be seen finally in an adult community, which is what is envisaged of course in the third principle: *Dialogue makes it possible to share in service to the community.* Christians do not have a monopoly of service ideals, and the problems of our world need all the resources which we have to bring to bear on them. This can already begin in the school which is pluralist in composition and Christian in intent. If the great danger of the confessional school, whether Christian, Jewish or Muslim, is the isolation or 'ghettoization' of such youngsters, the emphasis on serving the whole community as a mixed company will surely alleviate the problem considerably.

Fourthly, *Dialogue becomes the medium of authentic witness* in ways which we have already touched on. There are perhaps two kinds of witness. There is a witness *with* people of other faiths, testifying to the dimension of transcendence in life, to the element of mystery which is wrapped up with our understanding of what is finally good and desirable, and to the consequent need for humility in the face of it, and of human attempts to speak about it adequately. In the famous words of Max Warren: 'Our first task in approaching another people, another culture, another religion, is to take off our shoes, for the place we are approaching is holy. Else we may find ourselves treading on men's dreams.' Our western ways are too abrasive, or too austere. We need this co-witness to human frailty and insignificance in the scale of divinity.

At the same time we have to witness *to* people of other faiths, testifying to the very significance God has endowed us within the person of Jesus, to the strength and purpose of the divine love expressed in him, which has become available to us through the wonder of his death and resurrection. The precise form of this testimony, its cutting edge, cannot be predicted, for people respond in different ways to the mystery of God's act in Jesus. If it were not so the 'active ingredient' could be isolated, turned into a principle and replicated in a multitude of instances in human theory and imagination. So we continue to point to him and to tell the story in the constant repayment of our endless debt of love.

Notes

1. See, for example, Cantwell Smith, W., *The Meaning and End of Religion*. New York, Macmillan, 1962.
2. 3rd edn London, Methuen, 1983.
3. It should be noted that 'Modern' is not equivalent to 'Western' in this scheme. Many working-class people in the West also preserve some 'Traditional' values.
4. See p. 122.

EIGHT

The Larger Issues:
Nationhood, Culture and Truth

Christopher Lamb was once invited to speak at an inner-city church men's group on the subject of Islam. The secretary, who had to introduce him, suddenly realized that he knew no more about him than his name, and asked in an agitated whisper: 'Do you belong to the English faith?' It was obvious what he meant and Christopher had no wish to make him more nervous than he was already, so he answered 'Yes, I'm a Christian'. But he could not help feeling a sense of betrayal of his Pakistani and African and Latin-American friends as he acquiesced in the identification of 'English' with 'Christian'. He knew too many who would question it from a multitude of viewpoints. Yet to the unsophisticated and untravelled person in England it is natural to claim Christianity as the faith of the English, at least historically. What was troubling this uncomplicated soul was the possibility that the evident Englishman who had come to speak about Islam was not in fact a Christian but a Muslim—an affront to all his categories.

If we are not to answer with the man who said that 'the creed of the English is that there is no God, and it is wise to pray to him from time to time', what are we to say about 'the English faith'? The asking of such a question may raise cultured eyebrows, but it will not go away. National communities need a faith to live by, a set of memories, a vision and a hope. For centuries the dominance of the institutional Church in England ensured that whatever private opinions were held here and there, 'religion' meant Christianity. John Hick quotes the novelist Fielding's Parson Thwackum: 'When I mention religion, I mean the Christian religion; and not only the Christian religion, but the Protestant religion; and not only the Protestant religion but the Church of England.' Earlier than the eighteenth century even the word 'religion' would not have been used in that sense, and the dominance of Christianity in one form or another was so complete as not even to be worth noting. What we have observed in the last two-and-a-half centuries is an accelerating emergence from what may be called 'implicit' religion, an uncritical, unselfconscious faith which has not needed to contrast itself with other faiths or no faith because it has not experienced at any depth their difference from or negation of its own. Those who worship when others worship, make holy-day when others make holy-day, fast when others fast may be said to share in the 'piety of the environment'. The villages of India and Pakistan preserve today the piety of a Hindu or Muslim environment. There is no need to make a decision to observe Ramadhan or Diwali, for everybody is doing it. It is as much part of the annual cycle of events as the sowing and the harvest. No-one plans for it.

All over the world, of course, this unspoken consensus is breaking down under the pressure of urban and industrial change. Everywhere we see the emergence of autonomous individuals who sit loose to the traditional family and social ties, who sleep in one place, work in another and take their leisure in a third, changing their ethics as they change their clothes. For many such people the traditional religious observances become vestigial, something to be done on return visits home, or when the cycle of birth, marriage and death calls for the traditional rites of passage. Others, more devout or perhaps more insecure, take their faith with them into the new existence but find that special provision needs to be made for its expression. Now that the yearly round does not necessarily provide stimulus for fast and festival, and children do not learn to worship by simple observation and imitation it becomes necessary consciously to arrange for the observance and transmission of the faith. From the piety of the environment we pass to the piety of the sect. People become articulate for the first time about what they believe, and are increasingly aware of themselves as standing for different things from those of other belief or no belief. Even when, as with Hinduism, the prevailing philosophy emphasizes the essential unity of all religions, the fragmentation of urban life is producing something akin to the denominational pattern of western Protestantism among Hindus, especially those living in the West.

We have over-simplified, of course, but the distinction between the two types of piety may help to make sense of the remark about 'the English faith'. The man who made it was expressing, even in inner-city Birmingham, the piety of the environment, the sense that a certain way of life marches hand-in-hand with a certain way of worshipping. For him it would no doubt be important to preserve both. So many inner-city churches in multi-faith areas are supported by people — some of whom travel in from other areas to the place where they grew up — who feel instinctively that they are doing something to keep English culture alive in an environment which has become bewilderingly alien. There is a particularly fierce loyalty to church buildings as the visible symbol of this struggle, and a corresponding resentment when proposals are made to dispose of them, especially to people of another faith.

It is important to distinguish these attitudes from racism. Patriotism, to which they are so closely related, is not racist at heart, although of course Fascist organizations have always tried to harness patriotism to their own purposes and have often succeeded in deceiving decent people for a time. 'The English faith' kind of person can in one sense be said to be resisting the narrowing of his religious understanding into the piety of the sect. It is for him a broader, though less articulate thing. It is somehow 'English'. The implications of this are very extensive indeed. On the one hand it points to a communal and social bond which releases faith from being a merely personal, quirky thing, and the Church a collection of odd individuals who enjoy a peculiar kind of weekly meeting. That wider dimension is immensely important in sustaining the supporters of tiny, elderly congregations meeting in dilapidated premises. At best 'Englishness' roots faith in specific tasks and loyalties.

The problems, however, of 'the English faith' idea are twofold. First, in what sense can England (leave alone the rest of the United Kingdom) be said to adhere to Christianity as the national faith? In the context of sectarian religion could any faith anywhere be so described? Even in the self-styled

Islamic Republic of Pakistan there have been intense struggles between Sunni and Shi'ite protagonists over the content of Islamic teaching in schools, each claiming that theirs is the true Islam. (It is interesting to note that these clashes have come to a head *since* the programme of 'Islamizing' the laws and institutions of the country was begun.) Secondly, if Christianity can properly be described as the English faith, does not this prove that religious adherence is culturally conditioned and that all claims to finality (which are particularly characteristic of Christianity and Islam) should be abandoned? We are Christians, as others are Muslims, because we were taught to be so. 'The English faith' is no more than a habit of mind. A moment's thought, however, will show that those two objections are mutually contradictory. If no faith can be described as the national faith then we have already moved into a 'sectarian' type of piety, and people have begun, at least, to think out the implications of their faith, and to grapple with its claims to finality. But secondly, does the fact that one religion, whether it be Christianity or Islam, is socially dominant affect in any way its claim to truth? Hinduism or Buddhism may be as all-pervasive as the air you breathe but does that of itself determine the judgements we will want to make in theology? How can the fact that millions of people believe something make it true or untrue?

However, sociology cannot be ignored, and the theory of religious cultural conditioning does at least take the inescapable cultural plurality of our world seriously. In a more sophisticated form the theory goes something like this: (we are greatly indebted here to George Lindbeck's work *The Nature of Doctrine: Religion and Theology in a Postliberal Age*[1], both for his ideas and his terminology): There is, so many claim, a basic and universal experience, found in every cultural and racial community in the world, which we call 'religious experience'. Definition is extraordinarily difficult, but includes a sense of the transcendent, or numinous, or God, often understood as a personal being. The believer longs to enter into the condition characterized by this transcendence, and his attempts to do so produce a variety of rituals, holy artefacts and writings, and personnel who specialize in the appropriate activities. Certain places are also closely associated with these experiences. These religious experiences, it is believed, give rise to symbolic expressions of faith which may eventually become codified into a systematic 'doctrine' or 'theology'. But these formulations of thought are essentially expressions of experience rather than revelations of truth. The experience is primary and universal, but the expressions of it will naturally be culturally determined and therefore different from place to place and age to age. The philosophy or ideology of a faith has to be understood in terms of its own environment, and its claims to truth assessed within the terms provided by the culture. They have no necessary wider relevance. Lindbeck calls this the *Experiential/Expressive* view of doctrine, and it is briefly illustrated by a passage from a recent book by Wesley Ariarajah:

> When my daughter tells me that I am the best daddy in the world, and there can be no other father like me, she is speaking the truth. For this comes out of her experience. She is honest about it; she knows no other person in the role of her father. The affirmation is part and parcel of her being . . . But of course it is not true in another sense. For one thing, I myself know friends who, I think, are better fathers than I am. Even more importantly, one should be aware that in the next house is another little girl who also thinks that her daddy is the best father in the whole world. And she too is right . . . For here we are dealing not with absolute truths, but with the language of faith and love . . . The language of the Bible is also the language of faith. Whether we are speaking about the chosen people, or about Jesus as the only way, we are expressing a relationship that has profound meaning and significance for us . . . The problem begins when we take these confessions in the language of faith and love and turn them into absolute truths . . . Such claims to absolute truth lead only to intolerance and arrogance and to unwarranted condemnation of each other's faith-perspectives.[2]

It is not difficult to feel the attraction of such a viewpoint in the contemporary world, with its urgent need for mutual understanding and reconciliation. But it is also not difficult to see the difference between this understanding of faith, which originated essentially in the Enlightenment, and what

Christians have traditionally understood as the universal significance of Jesus. The vast majority of contemporary Muslims would make similar claims for the revelation enshrined in the Qur'an, brought through the 'Seal of the Prophets', Muhammad. For these traditional believers the doctrines of the faith are universally valid, truth-affirming propositions. They are not merely expressions of loyalty, devotion or intent to live in a certain way, though properly understood they involve all these things. They are also, and importantly, statements of how things are, 'first-order propositions', which are true in whatever culture they are expressed, and for whoever hears them. The only question is whether people will hear and obey. In the terminology developed by Lindbeck, this second view is the *Cognitive/ Propositional* understanding of the nature of doctrine. Over against the first view it has a clear and precise series of explanations about the fundamental truths concerning the world, life and human destiny, and an unfudged prescription about where everyone's ultimate loyalties should lie. In this way of thinking people are not locked into a culture-bound perspective like that of a little girl thinking about her father, but are free to move and, recognizing a greater truth, change their minds and leave their earlier loyalty.

The problem with this second Cognitive/Propositional understanding of religious language is that it tends to ignore cultural differences, not only geographically but also historically. The truth is fixed because it is revealed, and there is little room for learning from those who do not agree with you. Within Christianity it threatens to render impossible any ecumenical reconciliation between theologians of different traditions, since on this viewpoint the theologian cannot both be loyal to his tradition and at the same time admit that his ecumenical partner is saying the same thing. This problem still threatens the final success of the Anglican—Roman Catholic International Commission's work. As some see it, there can never be development in doctrine, only faithfulness or betrayal. The same situation exists in Islam, where the word often translated as 'heresy', *bid'at,* literally means 'innovation'.

Lindbeck offers a third viewpoint on doctrine, which he hopes will remedy the deficiencies of the other two, and which he calls a *Cultural/Linguistic* understanding. Here the basic analogy is that of language. Doctrine is like the grammar of faith, the unquestionable rules by which one lives and thinks. They are not purely arbitrary, for they have their own logic and their own order, but in the last resort it is not possible to explain them in other terms, or to say why, for example 'I think not it me fits good' is just not English, though all the words are. This view of doctrine clearly solves the problem of development, for languages constantly change and yet are recognizably the same. We also recognize that there are different ways of saying the same thing which carry different nuances in the same language. The analogy also deals with the *internal* issue of finality, and why it is in the end impossible to justify, e.g. the Lordship of Christ, except in terms drawn from Christian theology. In a very real sense every theology is a package deal, and insists on interpreting other theologies and other faiths in its own categories. This is just as true of Hindu and Buddhist thought as it is of Christianity and Islam.

At first sight it is less clear that Lindbeck's Cultural/ Linguistic approach has dealt with what we may call the 'external' problem of finality. After all we normally think of languages as, at least for normal business use, interchangeable. The United Nations conducts its affairs in six official languages; India manages to handle fourteen. If the same everyday meaning is conveyed through the use of totally different words, is it not likely that the very special expressions of religion also all speak ultimately of the same reality? It may be that the analogy of language simply breaks down here, but before we abandon it we should note that languages can and often do reflect *different* experiences. In learning Urdu/Hindi we were surprised to discover that one word serves to refer both to 'snow' and to 'ice'. The surprise only lasted however until we reflected that few among the millions of India and Pakistan have ever touched and handled snow for themselves. Similarly, as in other languages, almost all the technical vocabulary in engineering, even the simple words used when you take your car to the garage, are taken over virtually unchanged from English, since (as far as the Indian sub-continent is concerned) the 'engineering experience' is one which originates from England. More subtle frameworks of thought are also imprinted in language and surely come to determine how whole populations think. To use Urdu/Hindi examples again: the word for 'yesterday' and the word for 'tomorrow' are the same, which may reflect a cyclical understanding of history: you do not say 'I made a mistake' but 'A mistake happened to me', thus distancing yourself from any real responsibility for it: and you never say 'I have two brothers and one sister' but always include yourself in the enumeration, as 'We are three brothers and one sister' or 'We are two brothers and two sisters.' It is not difficult to discern whole philosophies thus embedded in the way people speak. In the last example the Indo-Pakistani formulation emphasizes the primary consciousness of the family unit, not of the individual who *has* brothers and sisters as he might possess a house and a car.

On this reckoning different languages not only reflect different experiences and the lack of them, but also interpret universal human experiences in profoundly different ways, suggesting different questions for faith to answer. This would need to be argued out at great length to be completely convincing, but already perhaps it is evident that the analogy with theological formulations is illuminating. But can it deal with the question of finality, or to use Lindbeck's term 'unsurpassability'? How does one deal in this way with the common claim that different faiths are neither better nor worse than one another but simply different, representing different facets of one transcendent reality? Or, in more agnostic vein, how does it deal with the claim that theological formulations of every kind may be internally coherent and even elegant without necessarily telling us anything about reality: without, in the technical language, providing us with 'first-order propositions'? This way of expressing the problem may actually lead us to a clue for solving it. If all faiths are equally right, then all faiths may be equally wrong. If all paths are said to lead to God, then it is just as possible that they all lead away from him. Faced with this alternative, most believers would point to the actual effects of religious beliefs in the lives and personalities of believers. It is not the speaking only but the *living out* of religious truth-claims which affirms them. Conversely the truth-claim may be denied at the moment of its being made if it is used to justify actions which are in themselves abhorrent. Lindbeck's example is the crusader's battle cry 'Christus est Dominus', which is false 'when used to authorize cleaving the skull of the infidel (even though the same words in other contexts may be a true utterance)'. Truth has to be *enacted* in order that a 'statement' may be made.

An example which may come more forcibly to mind is Christian treatment of the Jews, linked by Rosemary Reuther to Christian doctrine about Christ. 'Anti-Judaic thinking in the Christian tradition is the negative side of its christological hermeneutic', she wrote in her *Faith and Fratricide: The Theological roots of Anti-Semitism* (1974).[3] But is it? Or is it in fact a denial of Christian doctrines of Christ, not a denial in word, but a repudiation in fact and in blood, and all the more total for being so? Peter at Caesarea Philippi declared Jesus to be 'the Messiah, the Son of the living God', and Jesus told him that that had been revealed to him by God. But when Peter began to spell out what to *him* were the implications of the declaration, that Jesus was not to suffer persecution and death, Jesus called him Satan, and told him he thought as men think, not as God thinks. Peter's ambivalence has been with us ever since.

Another text of particular relevance here is the oft-quoted John 14.6, in which Jesus says 'I am the way; I am the truth and I am life; no one comes to the Father except by me'. The context of these words compels us to recognize that the 'way' of which Jesus speaks is the way of the cross which he is about to follow to the end. Here alone can be seen the truth about man and God, and from this alone the life of the resurrection can come. To quote this verse, then, cannot be simply to conclude an argument about other faiths. It must be primarily a statement of intent to embark upon the same way, insofar as we are enabled to follow it. 'When God calls a man,' wrote Bonhoeffer, 'he bids him come and die.' When, in hideous contrast, those who have called themselves Christians have set about procuring the deaths of others, John 14.6 is most convincingly denied. What we do about such perpetual denials in Christian history cannot be pursued here. Our first task is an unflinching recognition of them, even if we find ourselves driven to wonder whether Christians have ever really understood the gospel they proclaim. We are reminded (to use another example of Lindbeck) of non-physicists with no understanding of mathematics asserting that 'Space-time is a four-dimensional continuum'.[4] They may assert it correctly without knowing what it means. (This would certainly be so in our own case!)

It may be objected that religious, like scientific truth-claims must be examined independently of the status of the observer. We certainly do not wish to initiate an inspection of the moral qualities of the private lives of theologians. But even scientists now admit that the observer cannot help interfering with his own observation. The very fact and manner of making it alters the facts to be accounted for. To give a very prosaic example; when I check the tyre-pressures on my car, I can never know what the pressure *is*, only what it *was* before I let out a little air into the tyre-gauge. The process of making my observation alters what I observe. Even more evidently do the theories I hold, and the questions I ask in consequence, suggest different significant aspects of the material or phenomenon I am examining. We never come to any inquiry without some presuppositions, and we will not even be conscious of many of them.

We have wandered some way from the discussion of 'the English faith'. The significance of the viewpoint supplied by Lindbeck is that it takes seriously the inescapable plurality of world cultures, and yet suggests ways in which religious belief in its most definite and assertive form can be held without arrogance or dishonesty. To return to the analogy of language, we are toddlers lisping things which we have hardly begun to understand — as our history proves. Such a viewpoint for religious affirmation is available in principle for adherents of any faith (though hardly for those of none, if such genuinely exist). But there are particular reasons why it should be appropriate for Christians, and even more so for English Christians. The central affirmation of Christianity is that God entered human life in the person of Jesus, and through him brought about the reconciliation of humanity to himself. It follows that Christians are more concerned with a life than with a philosophy, with growth into the ways of God and a personal knowledge of him rather than blueprints for a new social and political order. This is not to say that sound thought and social ethics do not matter, only that in the perspective of Jesus we are children already beloved in him and are continuing to struggle with these things. 'I tell you, whoever does not accept the Kingdom of God like a child will never enter it.' Humility and repentance are always appropriate for the Christian, for he has already seen God's judgement on the world, and he knows that it begins with the household of faith. He cannot, like some Muslims, shout 'God is great' with a clenched fist. The crusading mind, as the Japanese theologian Kosuke Koyama has urged, must give way to the crucified mind.[5]

All this will be much too tentative for some who are deeply concerned both for the steep moral and economic decline of this country, and for the attenuated position of the Church within it. But there is no escaping the need for a new realism about both. That has to begin with repentance and humility both about our religious history as Christians of the West, and about our national history, particularly as an imperial power. When this note is sounded, the response is often a groan and the accusation that the people who are always running Britain down are at it again. 'Where is your patriotism?' The answer is that a true patriotism will neither idolize nor idealize the fatherland/motherland, but will take part in its affairs vigorously and with an open-eyed gratitude, a critical solidarity. All this is well explored and sharply posed in the Baptist theologian Keith Clements' book on the significance of Dietrich Bonhoeffer's life and thought for contemporary Britain, *A Patriotism for Today* (1984).[6] Bonhoeffer's deep love for the people and culture of his native country brought him back from the safety of the United States in 1939, and launched him into active conspiracy against the Hitler regime, involving him in activities which any government against whom they were directed could only regard as treasonable. Clements depicts with great clarity the gratitude Bonhoeffer felt for Germany and its achievements, and his understanding of his country as part of God's order for the world. But he did not make the mistake of thinking of it as part of God's permanent order (an 'order of creation' in his terminology), but as a context for a people's work and worship (an 'order of preservation'). As such it deserved his loyalty and even devotion, but an uncritical loyalty and a blind devotion ('the love that asks no questions') would destroy the fatherland and much more besides.

In the right kind of patriotism both gratitude and repentance are necessary. In the context of our concerns in this book, our real repentance at the grosser failures of the past, both abroad and more recently here, must be mingled with gratitude at the wealth of human resources now represented in this country, and at the opportunity for creating a community of unparalleled diversity in a relatively homogeneous and geographically restricted environment. Britain is not the United States or India, where the sheer size of the population and the scale of the territory accentuates regionalism and independence. Our size demands national coherence, and much talk of a multi-cultural community must be a contradiction in terms. The (now old) joke that 'today's Brummie wears a shamrock in his turban' underlines the way that all ethnic communities, including the English Caucasians, are being compelled to interact and create a common, though richly varied, culture. And despite appearances there is a common thread of memory and shared experience, for in speaking of the ethnic minorities of Britain it is largely true that 'they are here because we were there'. The common task is so to labour that the next generation may inherit a culture and a national community where there is mutual respect and forbearance, compassion for the weaker and more disadvantaged members, and a place and a significance for everyone. Is not this the longing which lies behind the figures for unemployment, urban deprivation and casual crime? There is an enormous task of national reconstruction which is not just economic and social, but in the proper sense ideological, concerned with attitudes and values.

In this task the fundamental resource is the Christian gospel. Or rather, to put it the other way round, it is only by aiming at the Christian gospel and the Kingdom it proclaims that we are likely to hit the lesser target of the reconstruction of the national society. It is not a case of imposing Christianity and Christian values on an unwilling nation. In present circumstances this is simply a fantasy, though if certain groups obtained power the fantasy might become a nightmare.

It is a question of understanding what we are aiming at.

In the past, national greatness has been defined in terms of military power and economic muscle. That ideal was always shallow, but in the nuclear age has been revealed as unforgivably dangerous. Past recipes for national greatness are disastrous for today, whoever pursues them. So what is greatness, national or other? The Muslim cry is that 'God is great' (literally greater than anything else you could name). We agree, but go on to ask, with Kenneth Cragg, how is he great? In what does his greatness consist? Using human analogies, is the greatness of God the greatness of the monarch, the judge, the general, the hero, the father, the teacher or the shepherd? It is ultimately from religious categories that the lesser, but still critical concerns of the nation and the human community are serviced. What is the controlling image of that which is great, and good and desirable, for men and women and for nations? There is no avoiding religious language and religious issues here, except by turning one's back on the future and taking refuge in nihilism or the myopic pleasure-seeking which is hardly less destructive.

It seems to us that Christians must not shrink from exploring their own tradition at much greater depth than in the past, and from commending it in every conceivable way as the instrument God has chosen for the well-being of the world. We do not need to pretend that our Christian history is more glorious or less squalid than it is. But we do need to assert that faith in the God made known in Christ is not just for those brought up in a particular culture and environment. Nor is it for those who are searching for a religious psychotherapy which happens to suit their own neuroses. Nor is it a Trojan horse for the capitalist domination of the world. God was in Christ reconciling the world to himself, and those who know themselves as his people do not promote themselves, but 'proclaim Christ Jesus as Lord, and ourselves as your servants, for Jesus' sake.' Such is all Christian ministry.

Notes

1. Lindbeck, G., *The Nature of Doctrine: Religion and Theology in a Postliberal Age* (SPCK 1984), p. 64.
2. Ariarajah, W., *The Bible and People of Other Faiths* (World Council of Churches 1985), pp. 25 – 7.
3. Reuther, R., *Faith and Fratricide. The Theological Roots of Anti-Semitism* (New York 1974), p. 64.
4. Lindbeck, op. cit., p. 66.
5. Koyama, K., *Waterbuffalo Theology* (SCM 1974), chapter 19; *No handle on the Cross. An Asian Meditation on the Crucified Mind.* SCM 1976.
6. Clements, K. W., *A Patriotism for Today. Dialogue with Dietrich Bonhoeffer.* Bristol Baptist College 1984.

Bibliography

In relation to the vast amount of material available this is inevitably a personal selection, slanted to the needs of a comprehensive British ministry. Thus we have omitted much that is of great value, but too technical, weighty or simply out of print and obtainable only in theological libraries. The latter, of course, will want much more than appears here, though we suspect that many may lack some of the items even of this modest list.

1. Reference

Hinnells, J. R. ed., *The Penguin Dictionary of Religions*. Penguin 1984. 550 pp.

A little complicated to use, but extremely helpful once you have mastered it, with extensive bibliographies and a section which groups articles in a 'Synoptic Index' according to faith. It aims at an academic 'objectivity' which raises many unanswered questions.

A Lion Handbook. The World's Religions. Lion Publishing 1982. 448 pp.

Lavishly and skilfully illustrated in the Lion manner, this aims to provide an objective account of world faiths from a Christian standpoint, reckoning no contradiction need be involved thereby. Text, pictures and diagrams are vivid, but sometimes misleading.

Bishop, P. D., *Words in World Religions*. SCM 1979. 152 pp.

A much smaller work, setting out the principal terms of Hinduism, Jainism, Buddhism, Judaism, Islam and Sikhism under helpful sub-headings (e.g. 'Buddhism in Tibet').

2. Christian Theology

Christian theology itself has to be rethought with the multi-faith perspective in mind.

Faith in the City Report of the Archbishop's Commission. Church House Publishing 1985. 398 pp.

Cracknell, K., and Lamb, C., *Theology on Full Alert,* Revised and enlarged edition, BCC 1986.

The first provides much basic data. The second attempts to raise consciousness in places of ministerial training. But the problem goes back to the nature of theology itself. Here we have valued the following:

Hebblethwaite, B. L., *The Problems of Theology.* Cambridge 1980. 164 pp.

Lindbeck, G. A., *The Nature of Doctrine. Religion and Theology in a Postliberal Age.* SPCK 1984. 142 pp.

Both books understand other faiths as part of the raw material of theology. Lindbeck urges a move from understanding theological language as either 'propositional' (conservatives) or 'experiential/expressive' (liberals) to 'cultural/linguistic' (postliberals). This really does help.

Perhaps the most extensive rethinking has to be done in relation to Jewish understanding of Old and New Testament. This intellectual adventure is both enriching and disturbing:

Magonet, J., *Form and Meaning. Studies in Literary Techniques in the Book of Jonah.* Sheffield, The Almond Press, 1983. 184 pp.

Leech, K. ed., *Theology and Racism — 1.* Church of England Board for Social Responsibility 1985. 54 pp.

To hear a Rabbi on Jonah is to open a new world; to wrestle with the BSR document and its question of whether the New Testament itself is anti-Semitic is a painful but vital task. We must see, as Christians, that the New Testament has been *made* anti-Semitic and remains so in some minds, both Jewish and Christian. We never approach the Bible presupposition-less.

The Jewish dimension raises acute questions for Christology in particular. Christopher Lamb has taken a very brief look at these, concentrating on the meaning of Jesus's death in his *Jesus Through Other Eyes: Christology in Multi-Faith Context.* Latimer House, 131 Banbury Road, Oxford OX2 7AJ 1982. 36 pp.

Samuel, V. and Sugden, C., ed., *Sharing Jesus in the Two Thirds World.* Eerdmans 1983. 419 pp.

This is a much more technical discussion from a variety of cultural perspectives, particularly Latin-American. There is a fascinating essay from Ghana (Bediako) and a valuable one from the Islamic context (Nazir Ali), as well as material from Hindu and Buddhist countries.

Bailey, K. E., *Poet and Peasant* and *Through Peasant Eyes* described as 'Literary-Cultural Approach to the Parables in Luke' and combined in one edition. Eerdmans 1983. 238 and 186 pp. (Paternoster Press handle Eerdmans' books in the UK).

Here is an approach to hermeneutics which draws on immense experience of the Middle Eastern setting of Jesus's parables, but also from early Syriac and Arabic translations and commentaries — a much neglected source which can help to free us from our cultural captivity to western thought-forms.

Koyama, K., *Mount Fuji and Mount Sinai. A Pilgrimage in Theology.* SCM 1984. 273 pp.

Song, C. S., *Tell Us Our Names. Story Theology from an Asian Perspective.* New York, Orbis Books, 1984. 212 pp.

These and other books by both authors share Bailey's achievement of cultural liberation from the West. Koyama's account of the failure of Japan's pre-1945 ideology of 'Wealthy Nation Strong Army' has many implications for the similar American and 'Free West' ideology under which he now lives in New York. He sees both as essentially idolatrous, symbolized by the nature worship of Mount Fuji, and calls for a move to the worship of the God of history and judgement symbolized by Mount Sinai.

de Silva, L. A., *The Problem of the Self in Buddhism and Christianity.* (First published in Sri Lanka in 1975 with 160 pp. Macmillan 1979.)

Lynn de Silva was a great Methodist pioneer in Christian-Buddhist relations whose work is now bearing fruit in the attempts to heal Sri Lankan divisions. In this book he rejects the notion of the immortal soul—as Buddhists do—as unbiblical, but also finds the Buddhist concept of *anatta* (non-egocentricity) inadequate until coupled with *pneuma.* The social consequences of all this are surprisingly concrete and urgent.

3. Pastoral and Cultural Issues

Most of the relevant material here is in pamphlet or booklet form, much of it published by the British Council of Churches Committee for Relations with People of Other Faiths. An essential starting point is that Committee's
Relations with People of Other Faiths. Guidelines for Dialogue in Britain. Rev. edn, 1983. 24 pp.

Also of value are:

Lamb, C., *Mixed-Faith Marriage: A Case For Care.* BCC 1982. 12 pp. (See our Appendix D.)

Our Ministry and Other Faiths. A Booklet for Hospital Chaplains. CIO 1983. 33 pp.

Asians in Britain: Caring for Muslims and their families, Asians in Britain: Caring for Hindus and their families, Asians in Britain: Caring for Sikhs and their families. All 80+ pp. booklets available from the National Extension College, 18 Brooklands Avenue, Cambridge CB2 2HN.

Also with a medical slant is
Goodacre, D., ed., *World Religions and Medicine.* Institute of Religion and Medicine, 55 St Giles, Oxford OX1 3LU 1983. 76 pp.

Carver, G., *A Place to Meet. The Use of Church Property and the New Religious Minorities in Britain.* BCC 1978. 39 pp.

Holden, B., and Rolls, E., *Christian Community and Cultural Diversity.* National Centre for Christian Communities and Networks, Westhill College, Selly Oak, Birmingham B29 6LL 1982. 43 pp.

This unusual little book has an extremely useful resources section.

Lamb, C., *Belief in a Mixed Society.* Lion Publishing 1985. 160 pp.

Newbigin, L., *The Other Side of 1984. Questions for the Churches.* WCC 1983. 75 pp.

These both, in different ways, raise questions about our inherited culture while attempting to remain faithful to the God made known in Jesus. Christopher Lamb's is the more concrete, Bishop Newbigin's the more far-reaching discussion.

There are many solid academic studies on migration and its consequences, among them:

Anwar, M., *Pakistanis in Britain. A Sociological Study.* New Century Publishers 1985.

Littlewood, R., and Lipsedge, M., *Aliens and Alienists. Ethnic Minorities and Psychiatry.* Penguin 1982. 278 pp.

'Is it possible' ask the authors 'that religion and mental illness may both be alternative responses to the same situation?' What is 'normal'? What *feels* normal to people is revealed in

Bowker, J., *Worlds of Faith. Religious Belief and Practice in Britain Today.* BBC 1983. 312 pp.

These are transcripts of interviews with ordinary British Jews, Muslims etc., not theologians, but the Professor of Religious Studies at Lancaster University has organized the material very usefully.

4. Educational Issues

As teachers are in the forefront of dealing with the consequences of a multi-cultural society there is a vast amount of relevant educational material, especially in RE.

Two valuable papers from the Church of England are available from its Board of Education:
Schools and Multi-Cultural Education. 1984. 46 pp.
A Future in Partnership. 1984. 112 pp.
A similar Roman Catholic document is
Learning from Diversity. A Challenge for Catholic Education.
  Catholic Media Office 1984. 86 pp.

The SHAP Working Party has an annual mailing on RE available from SHAP Mailing, Mr Peter Woodward, 7 Alderbrook Road, Solihull, West Midlands B91 1NH.

The same group has produced
Owen Cole, W., ed., *World Religions: A Handbook for Teachers.* 3rd edn, CRE, 1977. 205 pp.

Owen Cole, W., ed., *World Faiths in Education.* Allen & Unwin 1978. 190 pp.

Bailey, J., *Themework. Assembly Material for Junior, Middle and Lower Secondary Schools.* Stainer & Bell 1981. 229 pp.

This should help some teachers and others grappling with the agonies of school assembly, and the stories are a delight in themselves, though an Islamic dimension is seriously missing.

Palmer, M., and Bisset, E., *Worlds of Difference.* Blackie and the World Wildlife Fund 1985.

This is a fascinating project for schools examining the creation stories of different faiths and cultures and the lessons they hold for our treatment of our small planet. This is only one example of the way that the teaching of world faiths can spill over creatively from the RE classroom.

5. Mission and Dialogue

Here be dragons. For some it is the case for dialogue that has to be argued, for others it is mission and evangelism that is in question. Both, however, must listen to converts. Unfortunately most testimonies of conversion from another faith are haunted by the ghost-writer. Here are one that survived, and one that never needed, a ghost-writer:

Sheikh, B. (with Richard Schneider), *I Dared to Call Him Father.* Kingsway 1978.

Guinness, M., *Child of the Covenant. A Jew Completed by Christ.* Hodder 1985.

The Lausanne Occasional Papers have summarized the Pattaya, Thailand Conference of 1980:

No 6. *Christian Witness to the Chinese People.*
No 7. *Christian Witness to the Jewish People.*
No 13. *Christian Witness to Muslims.*
No 14. *Christian Witness to Hindus.*
No 15. *Christian Witness to Buddhists.*

Each paper is 20−30 pages long and is available from Whitefield House, 186 Kennington Park Road, London SE11 4BT.

Bi-lateral mission and dialogue are well served by these publications:

With Jews

United Reformed Church, *Christians and Jews in Britain. A Study Handbook for Christians.* URC, 86 Tavistock Place, London WC1H 9RT 1983. 96 pp.

Marmur D., *Beyond Survival. Reflections on the Future of Judaism.* Darton, Longman & Todd 1982. 218 pp.

The reflections of a liberal Rabbi on the state of his own faith-community — with implications for others!

Blue, L., *To Heaven with Scribes and Pharisees. The Jewish Path to God.* Darton, Longman & Todd 1975. 104 pp. —and other Blue books besides.

Solomon, Rabbi Dr N., *Jewish/Christian Dialogue. The State of the Art.* Inaugural lecture. Centre for the Study of Judaism and Jewish/Christian Relations, Selly Oak Colleges, Birmingham B29 6LQ 1984. 32 pp.

With Muslims

Christians and Muslims Talking Together (translated from the German by Kenneth Cracknell), BCC 1984. 106 pp.

A useful review of the issues from a European perspective —but somehow omitting the Atonement!

McDermott, M. Y., and Ahsan, M. M., *The Muslim Guide. For Teachers, Employers, Community Workers and Social Administrators in Britain.* The Islamic Foundation, 223 London Road, Leicester LE2 1ZE 1980. 104 pp.

A plea for people in authority over Muslims in Britain to recognize some basic Muslim needs.

Chapman, C., *'You Go and Do the Same'. Studies in Relating to Muslims.* CMS and BMMF International 1983. 92 pp.

Kateregga, B. D., and Shenk, D. W., *Islam and Christianity. A Muslim and a Christian in Dialogue.* Eerdmans 1981. 182 pp.

The authors taught together at Nairobi University and have set Christian and Muslim faith into a 2 x 12-point framework, each article of faith eliciting a response from the other believer.

Cragg, K., *The Call of the Minaret.* Collins 1986, 358 pp.

The Cragg classic—in a second edition after thirty years since its first publication.

Geijbels, M., *Muslim Festivals and Ceremonies in Pakistan.* Christian Study Centre, Rawalpindi, Pakistan 1982. 62 pp. Available from St Joseph's Bookshop, Lawrence Street, Mill Hill, London NW7 4JX.

A rare and scholarly account of how Islam is actually practised in Pakistan—the real 'folk Islam'.

With Hindus

Robinson, J. A. T., *Truth is Two-Eyed.* SCM 1979. 160 pp.

A tour de force by the late NT scholar, though heavily

dependent on Robin Boyd's *Introduction to Indian Christian Theology.* 2nd edn, Madras 1975—and still no British edition!

Hooker, R., *Journey into Varanasi.* 1978. 75 pp. and *Voices of Varanasi.* 1979. 119 pp. Both published by CMS.

Brown, J. M., *Men and Gods in a Changing World. Some themes in the Religious Experience of twentieth-century Hindus and Christians.* SCM 1980. 182 pp.

As the sub-title suggests, a book about experience rather than theology, but searching and perceptive about the resources of both faiths to cope with the stresses engendered in twentieth-century living.

Brockington, J. L., *The Sacred Thread. Hinduism in its Continuity and Diversity.* Edinburgh University Press 1981. 216 pp.

Probably the best introduction to the subject currently available.

Bowen, D. G., ed., *Hinduism in England.* Bradford College, Great Horton Road, Bradford 1981. 123 pp.

A collection of conference papers with the incoherence inevitable in a wide-ranging discussion, but so far the only thing of its kind for the British situation.

Guptara, P., *Indian Spirituality.* Nottingham, Grove Books 1984. 24 pp.

Guptara describes himself as 'a Hindu follower of Jesus', believing with Sadhu Sundar Singh that the Water of life must be presented to Indians in an Indian cup if they are to be expected to drink it.

With Sikhs

Cole, W. O., and Sambhi, P. S., *The Sikhs, Their Religious Beliefs and Practices.* Routledge & Kegan Paul 1978. 210 pp.

Cole, W. O., *The Guru in Sikhism.* Darton, Longman & Todd 1982. 115 pp.

James, A. G., *Sikh Children in Britain.* OUP 1974. 117 pp.

With Buddhists

Oliver, I. P., *Buddhism in Britain.* Rider 1979. 224 pp.

Johnston, W., *The Mirror Mind.* Fount Collins 1983. 181 pp.

6. Christian Theology of Religion

Cracknell, K., *Towards a New Relationship. Christians and People of Other Faith.* Epworth 1986. 198 pp.

D'Costa, G., *Theology and Religious Pluralism. The Challenge of Other Religions.* Blackwell 1986. 155 pp.

Hick, J., and Hebblethwaite, B., ed., *Christianity and Other Religions. Selected Readings.* Fount Collins 1980. 253 pp.

A very useful conspectus of twentieth-century views from Ernst Troeltsch to John V. Taylor, though only two non-westerners are included. It could already be up-dated with advantage.

Anderson, G. H., and Stransky, T. F., ed., *Mission Trends No 5 Faith Meets Faith.* Eerdmans 1981. 306 pp.

Anderson, G. H., and Stransky, T. F., ed., *Christ's Lordship and Religious Pluralism.* New York, Orbis Books 1981. 209 pp.

Towards a Theology for Interfaith Dialogue. CIO 1984. 40 pp.

Accepted as a basis for discussion by the Church of England but criticized in some Evangelical circles. See:

Sugden, C., *Christ's Exclusive Claims and Interfaith Dialogue.* Nottingham, Grove Books 1985.

These multi-authored documents may not have sufficient depth for those seriously battling with the issues, in which case:

Smith, W. C., *The Meaning and End of Religion.* SPCK 1978 (American edn 1962). 340 pp.

'The end of religion . . . is God. Contrariwise, God is the end of religion . . .' A profoundly influential study in the concept of 'religion', and the peculiar modern use which speaks of '*a* religion'.

Smith, W. C., *Towards a World Theology.* Macmillan 1981. 206 pp.

This begins where the earlier book left off (ch. 1 'A History of Religion in the Singular'), but, not surprisingly, reaches only an 'Interim Conclusion'. Enormously erudite, not an easy book.

Cragg, K., *The Christian and Other Religion. The Measure of Christ.* Mowbrays 1977. 138 pp.

Newbigin, L., *The Open Secret. Sketches for a Missionary Theology.* SPCK 1978. 214 pp.

Anderson, Sir N., *Christianity and World Religions. The Challenge of Pluralism.* IVP 1984. 216 pp.

Anderson, as ex-missionary, lawyer and Islamicist, brings unusual experience and vigour to the debate, singling out John Hick in particular for criticism in a thorough discussion of recent British thought on the subject.

Hick, J., *God Has Many Names. Britain's New Religious Pluralism.* Macmillan 1980. 108 pp.

Republished essays with an introduction on his 'spiritual pilgrimage' to his present position—a revealing description of how experience can affect theology even (especially?) in the academic.

Brown, D., *All their Splendour. World Faiths: the way to Community.* Fount Collins 1982. 222 pp.

The late Bishop of Guildford's last book, full of a passionate desire that we should see God's splendid creation brought into a unity in Christ. The title refers of course to Rev. 21.24.

Race, A., *Christians and Religious Pluralism. Patterns in the Christian Theology of Religions.* SCM 1983 176 pp.

Knitter, P. F., *No Other Name? A Critical Survey of Christian Attitudes toward the World Religions.* SCM 1985. 288 pp.
Two important surveys from a 'pluralist' perspective.

This bibliography ought perhaps to finish on a practical note with the question that many are asking in the light of all the debate above:

Can We Pray Together? Guidelines on Worship in a Multi-Faith Society. BCC 1983. 31 pp.

7. Some Relevant Journals

Discernment A journal of religious encounter, from BCC 2 Eaton Gate, London SW1W 9BL.

Interfaith News from 28 Powis Gardens, London W11. Thrice yearly.

World Faiths Insight from same address. Twice yearly.

Journal of the Evangelical Christians for Racial Justice from 12 Bell Barn Shopping Centre, Cregoe Street, Birmingham 15.

Current Dialogue from WCC.

International Bulletin of Missionary Research from PO Box 1308-E, Fort Lee, New Jersey 07024-9958, USA. Quarterly.

Newsletter and other publications from the Centre for the Study of Islam and Christian Muslim Relations, Selly Oak Colleges, Birmingham B29 6LE.

Update (on new religious movements) from The Dialog Center. Katrinebjergvej 46, DK-8200 Aarhus N, Denmark. Quarterly.

Some Relevant Church Committees

The British Council of Churches' Committee for Relations with People of Other Faiths—this Committee is part of the Conference for World Mission within the BCC.
Chairman: The Bishop of Stepney, the Rt Rev. Jim Thompson;
Secretary: The Rev. Kenneth Cracknell, 2 Eaton Gate, London SW1W 9BL (01-730-9611).

Since 1978 this group has worked with its energetic and gifted secretary to produce a series of booklets designed particularly for clergy and church leaders, notably the seminal *Relations with People of Other Faiths: Guidelines for Dialogue in Britain.* 2nd rev. edn 1983.

The United Reformed Church's Mission and Other Faiths Committee—part of the URC's Department of World Mission.
Chairman: The Rev. Roger Tomes;
Secretary: The Rev. John Parry, URC, 86 Tavistock Place, London WC1H 9RT (01-837-7661).

This committee was one of the first denominational committees and has been one of the most creative, sponsoring in particular a series of consultations between Christians and Jews, and in September 1984 the first Christian-Sikh meeting at a national level in Britain. Their publications include:
With People of Other Faiths in Britain. 1980.
Christians and Jews in Britain. 1983.

The Church of England has two bodies:

1. The Archbishops' Interfaith Consultants—first known from 1975 as the Consultants to the Archbishops of Canterbury and York on Interfaith Relations.

Chairman: The Bishop of Ripon, the Rt Rev. David Young; Secretary: The Rev. Canon Dr R. J. Hammer, 22 Midsummer Meadow, Inkberrow, Worcs. WR7 4HD.

The Consultants have among them a specialist on each of the major world faiths, and are currently working out a division of responsibilities with

2. The Interfaith Consultative Group—which reports to the Board of Mission and Unity of the General Synod.
Chairman: The Bishop of Bristol, the Rt Rev. Barry Rogerson; Secretary: Mrs Mary Tanner, BMU Church House, Dean's Yard, London SW1P 3NZ (01-222-9011).

This is the group which was primarily responsible for the report received and commended for study by the General Synod in July 1984, entitled *Towards a Theology for Interfaith Dialogue . . .* CIO 1984 (the little row of dots is part of the title and not an oblique comment of ours . . .).

The Methodist Church has a new committee as part of its Home Missions Division:

The Methodist Church Committee for Relations with People of Other Faiths.
Chairman: The Rev. Dr Donald English;
Secretary: The Rev. Martin Forward, 3 Byway Road, Leicester LE5 5TF.

The Methodist Church has previously published *Shall We Greet only our own Family?*

The Roman Catholic Bishops' Conference of England and Wales has:

The Committee for Other Faiths (of its Dept. for Mission and Unity).
Chairman/Convenor: The Rt Rev. Charles Henderson, Park House, 6A Cresswell Park, London SE3 9RD.

The Church of Scotland also has a relatively new committee, but uniquely names it:

The Committee on Relations with Israel and with People of Other Faiths.
Convenor: The Rev. John M. Spiers;
Secretary: The Rev. T. Kiltie, 121 George St, Edinburgh EH2 4YN.

The Evangelical Alliance, and its sister Evangelical Missionary Alliance are at this moment reviewing how best to monitor the other-faith issues in their committee structures, having been deeply concerned about them both in the context of urban ministry and of the Muslim world in particular. Further information from:

The Evangelical Missionary Alliance
The Rev. Stanley Davies (Gen. Sec.), 186 Kennington Park Road, London SE11 4BT (01-735-0421).

It should be noted that all these are umbrella and review bodies which do not engage as committees in dialogue or encounter with people of other faiths, but which are largely composed of people deeply so involved. Their aim is to feed their own hardly won experience into the deliberating bodies of the churches, and to provide guidance and information to those beginning such engagements. The theological convictions they hold have been shaped and tested in encounter with people and societies of another faith. Hence the recurrent, and quite proper emphasis on 'relations with people of other faiths' which often forms part of such a committee's title. An older generation would probably have designated such work as 'Mission to . . .' and remained unrepentant about the feelings of those so 'targeted' by someone else's mission. We believe we are right not to objectify people of other faiths in this way, and to begin, at least, with an emphasis on mutuality.

More People

In addition to such national church committees there are growing numbers of local and regional groups of various kinds.
   The Anglican diocese of Birmingham has a committee (again '. . . For Relations with People of Other Faiths') which is now in its fourth working year.

The Bible and Medical Missionary Fellowship (BMMF) have, through their Ministry Among Asians in Britain, developed a new resources centre in Bolton, based at St Paul's Church, Deansgate. It is currently open all day on Mondays and at other times by appointment. With a reference collection of several hundred books and leaflets it also stocks AVA for hire, and books and other materials both in English and Asian languages for sale. Further information from:

Mr George Skinner, 12 Woodsley Road, Bolton BL1 5QL (0204-46756).

The missionary societies have often been instrumental in bringing the resources of the Church overseas to bear on ministry among Asians in this country. Some, like BCMS, now receive regular requests for advice, and slowly a body of valuable experience is being built up.

An Anxiety

We feel, however, a personal anxiety that we are so far failing properly to work with the Christians of Asian background who are themselves citizens of this country. Some clergy from the Indian sub-continent have carried out a vital and effective ministry as expatriate workers (missionaries? mission partners?) here. But there are others, both ordained and lay, who are permanently settled, even born here, who often feel discrimination against them from within the Church as well as from society in general. (See *Faith in the City* — the Report of the Archbishop's Commission on Urban Priority Areas, Church House Publishing 1985, pp. 95 – 100, 361). Asian Christians are a minority within a minority. As white Christians we have to learn both to receive their ministry to us, and to enable it to others — whether the 'others' will be primarily their fellow-Asians or (which is just as likely) not. Two reference points here are:

The Association of Black Clergy.
The Rev. Pat Taylor, 39 Lees Rd, Hurst, Ashton-u-Lyme OL6 8DP.

Evangelical Christians for Racial Justice.
Officer: Mr Raj Patel, 12 Bell Barn Shopping Centre, Cregoe Street, Birmingham B15 2DZ (021-622-6807).

New Religious Movements of Indian Origin

We have made several passing references to New Religious Movements, of which a bewildering variety are now to be found in Britain. The first purpose of this Appendix is to offer some general comments on them. Our hope is that these may serve as a simple, if crude, frame of reference which may enable the minister to bring some order out of the apparent chaos which confronts him on the ground. Second, we offer brief thumb-nail sketches of five movements as example.

At once we face the familiar problem of vocabulary. The authoritative statements of most of these movements claim that they are not new at all. Their founders may be said to have discovered long-forgotten truths of ancient wisdom, or the movement concerned may be based on certain well-established elements of a 'main-line' tradition, as in the case of Krishna Consciousness. However, what we can say with confidence is that all these movements are comparatively new arrivals on the British scene, and therefore unfamiliar to most Christians. We refer here to movements which are of Indian origin and leave out of consideration groups such as Jehovah's Witnesses, Mormons or Moonies, on which information is readily available elsewhere.

Those who join the movements with which we are concerned here may do so from a variety of motives. They probably feel let down by, or dissatisfied with their own inherited religious tradition, which perhaps is too closely attached to the language and culture of the homeland. It may have become too politicized, or perhaps people feel that the soul has gone out of it. It may be too exclusive and condemnatory in its attitude to other religions and their followers.

Those who belong to traditional Asian religions have

normally been nurtured within and upheld by the piety of the environment, while those who join the new movements have changed, whether consciously or not, to the piety of the sect. They can often talk in vivid and articulate terms of their conversion experience. They will readily and indeed eagerly expound the main principles of their new allegiance to the enquiring outsider. They can probably supply pamphlets and books which describe the faith and its history in more detail.

At the head of most of these movements is a leader or guru who is a powerful figure of authority. He is held to embody the experience on which the movement is based. He takes all the important decisions which affect its common life, and sometimes those which affect the personal lives of its members as well. His followers may go and visit him at an annual assembly — usually at the headquarters of the movement in India. Sometimes he may spend time touring the main centres in India and across the world where his followers are to be found. A few of the leaders are women. Probably too the movement will publish a regular magazine or journal as a means of keeping in touch with its members. All this illustrates the fact that they no longer belong to a static face-to-face society in which everyone knows everyone else. They are now modern people, mobile, uprooted from tradition, and increasingly isolated from their fellows. Indeed at one level we can understand the new movements as ways of coping with the social and psychological needs created by this new way of living.

Modern people are usually aware of religious plurality in a way that their parents or at any rate their grandparents were not. As we would expect, the new movements enable their members to cope with this. The movements may claim, as is characteristic of most Hindus today, that all religions say the same thing anyway, or that their particular leader was vouchsafed an experience which is in fact ancient and universal. The literature of the movements often contains references to Jesus, though to a Jesus who is made use of to support, illustrate and perhaps even legitimate the particular claims of the movements concerned. There are similar references to Muhammad, the Buddha and other important 'main-line' religious figures.

The presence of these movements in Britain today raises a

number of questions for the churches: the first concerns the tension between social coherence and religious freedom. There is little doubt that our society, like many others, is becoming more fragmented. New groups, by their very existence, appear to undermine still further what is left of our unity. This is an especially pressing issue for Anglicans who claim in some way to be a national church. On the other hand some Free Churchmen see the issue in very different terms. They themselves had to struggle against a dominant Church of England in order to win the right to exist and live their own life. They see the struggle of the new movements for freedom and recognition as a reenactment of their own history.

But are there limits to tolerance? By what criteria can a Christian—or anyone else—evaluate a new religious movement? The first thing we can do is to eliminate the loaded word 'cult' from our vocabulary. The anti-cult movement in the churches can sometimes be as demonic as the very enemy against which it purports to be fighting. We would tentatively suggest three criteria for assessing a movement: first what does it do to its followers? Does it deliver them from evil? Some members of new movements will claim, for example, that they used to be on drugs and that the teaching and experience of the new movement saved them from their addiction. Does the movement make its members more kind, gentle and loving people? Do they develop a social conscience and activities to match it? Next, how easy is it to leave the movement once one has joined, and what are the methods of 'evangelism'? Are these honest and do they put undue pressure on people? But what is 'undue' anyway? Finally, what of the movement's leader? Does he (or she) point people beyond himself, or does he become an idol? Is he more interested in maintaining the organization and the power which leading it gives him, or does he really care for the deepest well-being of his followers and indeed of all people?

These criteria need to be applied with caution and humility. With caution because they are all of necessity very vague and beg hosts of questions, and with humility because they all apply with equal force to old religious movements including many churches. Indeed we can only safely apply them to others if we are continually applying them to ourselves in collective self-examination.

These criteria concern the right of a movement to exist in a reasonably open society such as ours. They say nothing about questions of truth or of Christian witness, and in any case these we have dealt with sufficiently in the body of the book. We would suggest, however, that these latter issues can only properly be raised if we are seriously engaged with the former.

We now offer brief sketches of five movements to serve as examples. In the remainder of this Appendix quotation marks indicate that the words between them are taken from the literature of the movement concerned.

1. Satya Sai Baba

This is the name of the movement's leader. He was born in 1926 in South India. It is claimed that 'even as a boy of 7 he composed hymns and wrote scripts and songs for religious dramas and morality plays. He "materialized" or produced from the air by a mere wave of his palm, objects like fruit, flowers and sweets for his comrades.' Many miracles of healing are attributed to him. His devotees claim that honey or, more frequently, ash (an important element in some Hindu religious rituals) flows from his pictures in their homes. His movement really began to spread in India and beyond in the 1960s, and now: 'Devotees of all religions go to him with great faith and are benefited. He says there is no need to change your chosen God and adopt a new one when you have seen Me and heard Me: for all names are Mine and all forms are Mine.

Baba says:

There is only one Race — the Race of Humanity.
There is only one Language — the Language of the Heart.
There is only one Religion — the Religion of Love.
There is only one God — God, the omnipresent.'

In sum, the appeal of Satya Sai Baba is to unity, to love and to the miraculous. He has a large and probably growing number of Hindu devotees in Britain, and some western ones as well.

2. Brahma Kumaris World Spiritual University

This movement began in 1937 in what is now Pakistan. Later, its headquarters moved to Mount Abu in the state of Rajastan in Western India. Its branches in Britain are usually called Raja Yoga Centres. The movement's teaching stresses that the world is on the brink of disaster. The only remedy for this is the inward transformation of humanity. We have to purify ourselves so that our souls return to their pristine and original undefiled state. Therefore the devotees, who may belong to any race, religion or nationality, practise vegetarianism, celibacy, and meditation. This, they say, can re-establish the Golden Age, and bring peace to humanity. God, on whom devotees meditate, is understood as a point of light which is to be found in all religions, as is the oval shape in which the light is located—the Shiva *linga,* or phallic emblem, of Hinduism, the Sacred Heart of Jesus, the centre of the Kaaba Stone at Mecca. God is addressed as Baba—Daddy—which implies a more intimate relationship than Father, 'though he is in truth the Father of us all'. The present leaders of the movement are two women, and throughout there has been a strong emphasis on the dignity and humanity of women. The movement is affiliated to the United Nations as a non-Governmental Organization.

3. Radha Soami Satsang

This popular sect is based at Beas, near Amritsar, in the Punjab, where it began in 1891 (having split off from an earlier movement which started in another part of India). At its heart is a succession of living gurus or Great Masters who are believed to possess sacred knowledge. This knowledge enables us to escape from the limits which beset our human state, and so to escape from the continuous cycle of rebirth which is our lot. The sacred knowledge and its possessor are one, so that the holy person is not distinct from the knowledge which he is held to possess. There are four dimensions, or realms of being, in the universe, of which man is a microcosm. Therefore these realms are also inwardly present in us all. Our aim must be to attain the highest realm, which the Great

Masters embody in their own persons. All this teaching is characteristically and profoundly Hindu. The movement is strictly vegetarian, it considers outward symbols and rituals to be unimportant, and holds that the teaching of the Great Masters underlies all religions. Claims of exclusiveness made by Christians, and others, are strongly rejected. Most of the members are Punjabis but there are also many western devotees as well. Many of the Great Masters' addresses are published in English (including a commentary on John 1 – 17) and these are held in great reverence.

4. Sant Nirankari Mission

This movement also began in what is now Pakistan, in 1929. Most of its members crossed the border into India in 1947. Like some of the other movements it stresses the importance of a line of living gurus. It claims to be 'not a religion or a sect, but a spiritual movement'. It is a way of leading a virtuous life while remaining devoted to the formless God. This Mission endeavours to establish Universal Brotherhood by inculcating non-violence, love, truth and spiritual awakening through God-realization. It is one vast human family of people from different castes, communities and religions. The mission firmly believes in the fundamental truth that (the) 'Formless God is the Creator, Sustainer and Liquidator of the universe.' It claims that a wrong emphasis on external rituals led to the formation of separate religions, and this has led to division and bloodshed. True religion, embodied in the person of its Guru, is inward and spiritual. Many of the movement's members are former Sikhs. Moreover, the claim that there is a continuous succession of Gurus down to the present is unacceptable to Sikhs, for whom the last human Guru was Guru Gobind Singh who died in 1708. This and other differences has led to violent clashes and indeed the fourth Nirankari Guru was murdered by Sikh extremists in India in 1980. This sad event illustrates a general principle: a movement which uses the sources and symbols of a main-line tradition in ways which are unacceptable to the guardians of that tradition will provoke more opposition than a movement which is altogether separate. For example, Christians are commonly more hostile to Jehovah's Witnesses than they are to any of the movements considered in this Appendix. There are, of course, often other and more profound reasons for hostility.

5. International Society for Krishna Consciousness

By contrast to the movements which we have so far considered this one does put a heavy emphasis on outward rites and symbols, and on diet and dress. It is based on a living stream of the main Hindu tradition. Its devotees are mainly western. Its philosophy is conveniently set out in one of its own pamphlets:

> The International Society for Krishna Consciousness (ISKCON) is a world-wide community of devotees practising *bhakti-yoga,* the eternal science of loving service to God. The Society was founded in 1966 by His Divine Grace A. C. Bhaktivedanta Swami Prabhupada, a pure devotee of God representing an unbroken chain of spiritual masters originating with Lord Kṛṣṇa Himself.
>
> The following eight principles are the basis of the Kṛṣṇa consciousness movement. We invite everyone to consider them with an open mind and then visit one of the ISKCON centres to see how they are being applied in everyday life.
>
> 1. By sincerely cultivating a bona fide spiritual science, we can be free from anxiety and come to a state of pure, unending, blissful consciousness in this lifetime.
>
> 2. We are not bodies but eternal, spirit souls, parts and parcels of God (Kṛṣṇa). As such, we are all brothers, and Kṛṣṇa is ultimately our common father.
>
> 3. Kṛṣṇa is eternal, all-knowing, omnipresent, all-powerful, and all-attractive. He is the seed-giving father of all living beings, and He is the sustaining energy of the entire cosmic creation.
>
> 4. The Absolute Truth is contained in the *Vedas,* the oldest scriptures in the world. The essence of the *Vedas* is found in the *Bhagavadgita,* a literal record of Kṛṣṇa's words.
>
> 5. We should learn the Vedic knowledge from a genuine

spiritual master—one who has no selfish motives and whose mind is firmly fixed on Krsna.

6. Before we eat, we should offer to the Lord the food that sustains us. Then Krsna becomes the offering and purifies us.

7. We should perform all our actions as offerings to Krsna and do nothing for our own sense gratification.

8. The recommended means for achieving the mature stage of love of God in this age of Kali, or quarrel, is to chant the holy names of the Lord. The easiest method for most people is to chant the Hare Krsna *mantra:*

> Hare Krsna Hare Krsna
> Krsna Krsna Hare Hare
> Hare Rāma Hare Rāma
> Rāma Rāma Hare Hare

Mixed-Faith Marriage:
A Case for Care

by Christopher Lamb

Marriage in Britain

For many years Christian clergy in Britain have faced the task of preparing for marriage an unending stream of couples who in many cases have little or no understanding of the Christian faith, and for whom their wedding is a rare contact with their local church. This has been particularly the case for the Church of England and Church of Scotland clergy, but in varying degrees for others also. Many valiant attempts have been made to conduct both preparation for marriage and the wedding itself in a way which will be meaningful to the couple and their circle of relatives and friends, and also authentically Christian, so that some Christian message and experience may be associated with the day.

In other cases the wedding has been the climax of a childhood and youth spent in the fellowship of the local church, and the minister at the wedding can assume a deep understanding of the gospel and its implications for marriage.

Mixed Marriage

In the new situation created by the presence of substantial numbers of people of Muslim, Sikh and Hindu faith in Britain, there are often occasions when the clergyman is faced with a baptized Christian, whether of his own congregation or not, who wishes to marry a person who is not simply an unbeliever, agnostic or indifferent, but actively the member of another faith. As more and more people of other faiths are born in this country, rather than entering it by immigration, and fully share in the life and culture of Britain, we can expect such mixed-faith marriages to increase considerably.

Viewed exclusively from a cultural point of view the Churches should surely welcome such signs that a multi-cultural society is here to stay, that the riches of Asian and African and Caribbean culture will be united with a traditionally British inheritance in the intimacy of marriage and family life in a way which will ensure new depths of insight and experience in the future people of this country. Though marriages across racial or cultural barriers will usually be subject to some tension in the meeting of different values and assumptions, that very tension can be extremely creative of new tolerance, understanding and personal growth. The organization HARMONY is dedicated to celebrating the advantages of racially or culturally mixed marriages and praising their children as privileged rather than as pitiable 'half-castes'.[1] If the roots of racial prejudice are to be found in the idea of racial purity then the mixed-race marriage is a determined blow for freedom, and the marriage of Christians of mixed race a sign of the gospel.

Mixed-Faith Marriage

But the issue of mixed-*race* marriage is not at all the same as the issue of mixed-*faith* marriage. The distinction is not always clear to people for many marriages are both. 'Mixed marriages celebrate love which defies race, religion and culture' says one writer.[2] It is vital we should be clear about the distinction in contemporary Britain where an Asian Christian or a white British Muslim is a comparative rarity, and where a Christian minister can be asked 'Do you belong to the English faith?'

In November 1980 the members of a church, a synagogue and a mosque congregation came together to discuss the growing incidence of mixed-faith marriages. Each faith-community had its own reasons for regretting the practice. For some it was the betrayal of the community, for some the betrayal of the faith, which hurt. But all agreed that such marriages were in fact increasing, in spite of the opinions of religious leaders.

The Biblical Background

It is important for Christians to consider carefully whether and in what ways they may regret mixed-faith marriages. Joseph, Moses, David and Solomon married non-Israelite women, but Deuteronomy 7. 3—4 forbids the practice because of the idolatry foreign wives introduced into the home. Ezra insisted on the dissolution of such marriages (chs 9, 10), and Nehemiah tore out the hair of offending Jews and cursed them (13.23 ff). (See also Malachi 2.10.) But the Old Testament also celebrates the marriage of Boaz and Ruth the Maobitess whose descendant was David. The Song of Songs may also be written in praise of a mixed-faith marriage. ('I am black but lovely, daughters of Jerusalem', 1.5, JB). It must be noted, however, that Ruth declared to Naomi 'Your people shall be my people and your God my God . . . I swear a solemn oath before the LORD your God: nothing but death shall divide us' (Ruth 1.16—17, NEB).

In the New Testament only Paul refers to mixed-faith marriages, when he counsels those who are already married to unbelieving partners at the time of their conversion (1 Cor. 7. 12—16). They should, he reckons, be ready to continue in such a marriage unless the unbelieving partner wants a separation or divorce, because 'the unbelieving husband is consecrated through his wife, and the unbelieving wife is consecrated through her husband'. A second marriage, however, should be *'en Kurio'*—'in the Lord' (RSV, JB) 'within the Lord's fellowship' (NEB), 'only if he is a Christian' (TEV). 2 Cor. 6.14 may or may not refer to marriage directly: 'Do not be mismated with unbelievers' (RSV); 'Do not try to work together as equals with unbelievers' (TEV).

But Paul's teaching about the relationship of Christ and the Church (Eph. 5.22 ff) as mirrored in the experience of marriage suggests that the intimacy of that marital relationship must also include the intimacy of a shared faith. Similarly when he warns against fornication he says that 'The two become one flesh' but that anyone joined to the Lord is 'one spirit with him'. (1 Cor. 6.16, 17). It would be strange for someone who is 'one spirit' with the Lord to become 'one flesh' with a partner who is not.

Christian Practice

The Church as a whole has proceeded on the assumption that Christians will marry Christians. From the earliest times the marriage ceremony was accompanied by a Eucharist (still echoed in the term 'wedding breakfast' where the couple break their pre-nuptial fast), and the language of the service has always been trinitarian. However, the Church has also insisted at all times that marriage was a sacrament conducted by the couple themselves, and that the Church's role was to be a witness before God and society to the solemnity of the vows undertaken. In other words marriage belongs essentially to the order of creation rather than that of redemption. Marriage did not originate with the Church, as Baptism and the Eucharist can be said to have done, and so perhaps its marriage discipline can be regarded as of the *bene esse* rather than of the *esse* of the Church.

But such considerations would be difficult to explain to the couples who come to so many parish clergy in contemporary Britain with minimal understanding of marriage and the faith itself. Such young people are often immediately concerned with the externals of clothes and choirs and guests. Clergy may see little difference between the nominal adherence of baptized but uncommitted Church 'members' who come for marriage in church, and the young person whose family and cultural origins are from another faith altogether. Here it is important to review the understandings of the other faith-communities in Britain about mixed-faith marriages.

The Practice of other Communities

The *Jewish Community* is deeply alarmed at the erosion of its own community in Britain through its members marrying outside the faith, and it has been calculated that some 30 per cent of Jews are now marrying non-Jews in Britain. Despite the understanding (from the Halachah) that Jewish identity is transmitted through a Jewish mother, it seems that most Jews regard the descendants of mixed-faith marriages as 'lost to Judaism'. This may yet produce a return to Jewish attitudes which attempt to 'protect' young Jews from non-Jewish influences.

Muslims have traditionally permitted the marriage of a Muslim *male* with a non-Muslim, preferably a Jew or a Christian, but there is some pressure from Muslim communities in Britain for the non-Muslim bride to accept Islam. This is felt to be a better safeguard in a situation where Muslims are open to many non-Muslim influences. But what is generally insisted upon is the prohibition of a Muslim *girl* marrying outside the faith, for it is feared that she will have to tolerate abuse of the Prophet and Islam, and be unable to bring up her children as Muslims. In some countries operating under Islamic laws such marriages are invalid in law, and the marriage of a Muslim couple may be automatically dissolved if the husband is converted to another faith.

The general *Hindu* practice of marriage within the caste is too well-known to need elaboration, but in Britain the characteristic Hindu 'tolerance' for all forms of religion may appear to present fewest obstacles to a mixed-faith marriage. Theological objections to a Hindu-Christian marriage are likely to be greater from the Christian side.

In *Sikhism* there is also a tradition of marriage within the kinship group and antipathy to Sikhs marrying non-Sikhs, for as the Guru Granth Sahib says 'They are not man and wife who have physical contact only. Only they are truly wedded who have one spirit in two bodies' (quoted in Cole & Sambhi: *The Sikhs: Their Religious Beliefs and Practices,* RKP 1978, p. 116). However it is possible for those outside the community to become Sikhs, and there is some evidence to suggest that this is preferred by the Sikh community in Britain, when a mixed-faith marriage is in prospect.

The *Buddhist* community is not large in Britain, and since in Buddhist and Chinese religious traditions it is possible to have more than one religious allegiance (Christmas Humphreys, a leading British Buddhist, said 'I call myself a Christian') there is presumably little difficulty from the Buddhist side about a mixed-faith marriage in itself, although the vegetarianism and pacifism of strict Buddhist life may present difficulties to Muslims and Jews, and to some Christians.

Other Assumptions

It is not possible here to detail the differing understandings of marriage itself in the various faith-communities, and since what matters is the particular attitude of the persons concerned it seems best to suggest questions that ministers should have in mind as they come to counsel young people who are considering a mixed-faith marriage. They are bound to take very seriously one *cultural* factor which nevertheless has its important *religious* implications, namely that in most Asian families marriage is a unity of the families as well as of the couple. This has great strengths in the traditional situation where families will work together to guide and counsel a couple whose marriage is showing signs of strain, and will at all times provide material support and care. Where a mixed-faith marriage is in prospect both families may have serious reservations about it, and therefore fail to provide the support which the Asian partner at least has always experienced from the family. They may even desire eventually to see the marriage fail, and be prepared to use the different religious allegiance to fuel prejudice against the other-faith marriage partner. Alternatively they may regard the marriage as an extension of the faith-community, and try to insist on the conversion of the partner to their faith, arguing that the marriage will be more secure that way.

It must also be remembered that in some religious traditions marriage is a contract, officially between two people, but effectively between two families, and that its ending may be anticipated and specifically allowed for in detailed arrangements about property at the time of the marriage. This inevitably detracts from the sense of permanence with which Christians approach a marriage. Often too the children of any marriage are thought of as belonging to the husband's family, and in some countries custody of the children will be given to his family rather than to his widow in the event of his death. This may be of importance if the couple eventually settle in the husband's country of origin, as will other issues like divorce and inheritance, (e.g. a Muslim cannot inherit from a non-Muslim and vice-versa).

Typical Situations

Here it may be helpful to consider some brief case-studies of typical situations:

a) Dawn, a member of the local church choir, goes out with Ali, born of a Bangladeshi Muslim family in this country and finally agrees to marry him. His family accept her happily, though she has some difficulty in conversing with his mother, who speaks almost no English and rarely leaves the house. Local Muslim opinion seems to be divided: some saying it is quite all right for a Muslim boy to marry a Christian girl (though not the reverse), while others think that she should become a Muslim. Dawn herself is torn between a willingness to become a Muslim for the sake of Ali, though she is not sure what that would mean, and the familiar ties of the Church. She always wanted a church wedding. She hopes that in some way she can do both.

b) An English woman marries a Muslim of Pakistani origin. At the time of their marriage neither party takes religion with much seriousness and the difference of faith seems to be unimportant compared with the other adjustments necessary. But they are happy. After several years of marriage the husband is strongly influenced by a revival movement centred in the local mosque, and begins to spend many hours there. At the same time his elder brother arrives from Pakistan and suggests that the children would be educated in a much less permissive moral climate if they were to go to school in Pakistan. He is prepared to take all responsibility for them. The husband feels he is right, and anyway is accustomed to obeying his elder brother as the head of the family, but the wife is deeply distressed.

c) An Englishman marries a Hindu girl. His background is Baptist, but he has dropped out of the church community and no longer worships regularly anywhere. Their first child is the occasion of great rejoicing, and recalls both parents to the mystery of life and procreation. Each wants to mark the birth with a ceremony expressing their sense of wonder. He wants a Christian dedication and naming ceremony (not baptism), and she wants the full Hindu rite. They approach the local Anglican vicar, and request a dedication service, adding on impulse that it would be nice if the Hindu priest could take part as well.

d) An English student couple live together without any intention of marriage. A child is born to them, and shortly after the boy becomes a Muslim. After a time his Muslim friends reprimand him for continuing to live with his girl without marrying her, and counsel him to marry her or leave her. He leaves her temporarily but makes it clear he wants to marry her if she will become a Muslim. She is confused about him, about marriage and about Islam, but is concerned for her child. What she has understood about the Christian faith now comes back to her, and she tries to find a counsellor who knows something about Christianity and Islam. First she tries her local church.

Note: At present it is not common for a white Christian man to marry a wife of another faith. Such marriages do occur, but they are unusual since it is a widespread Asian custom to regard the girl as the bearer of the family honour, and to prevent her, wherever possible, from making any relationship which might lead to such a marriage. No doubt Asian girls will in time be more involved in mixed-faith marriages, but today such girls risk rejection from their own families.

The Pastoral Task

What is the pastoral task of the Christian minister in such cases? Clearly much will depend on how he becomes involved in the situation; whether parents contact him in the hope that he will prevent such a marriage, or the couple in the hope that he will conduct their wedding ceremony or bless their child, or whether a member of his own congregation proposes to adopt the faith of his or her fiancé(e).

The task demands considerable pastoral, theological and psychological skills and it will take some experience to acquire them. A male pastor will do well to enlist the co-operation of a well-qualified and experienced Christian woman and vice-versa. Some general principles may be suggested:

1. A Pastor's main responsibility is to his church members

Can a minister do other than counsel a church member *against* marrying someone who does not share his or her faith? It is true that Christian history has many examples of Christian wives who were powerful influences for good on their unbelieving husbands, and some Christian queens like Bertha of Kent and Helen the mother of Constantine even became the human agents of the conversion of an entire nation. Their story needs to be told. But they were women who had no say in the disposal of their own hand in marriage, who were counters in a diplomatic exchange. In the circumstances of marriage today it would be foolish for anyone to enter it with the private intention of converting their unbelieving partner to their own faith. Still less will a minister easily accept the proposal that the Christian partner should adopt the faith of the other.

2. Pastors need to have a care for the spiritual integrity of all involved

This will mean for example that people should not be encouraged to go through with a form of words which can mean nothing to them, or with which they may actually disagree. This will apply both to the Muslim or Jew who offers to take part in a Christian marriage service where prayer is offered in the name of the *Trinity* and of Jesus, and to those Christians who offer to convert to another faith for the sake of their marriage partner. Even if the couple insists, or attempts to insist on participation in the—e.g. Anglican service of Holy Matrimony, it is probably wise to follow the recommendation of the bishops and ask them to be married by a civil ceremony which can be immediately followed by a specially devised service of prayer. It may be argued that many nominally Christian couples use words in such a marriage ceremony which they do not fully understand or accept, but it must be reckoned that an unbaptized person from a Muslim or Jewish background is part of a distinct alternative to Christianity in a way that the former are not. He or she belongs to a community where the characteristic Christian forms of prayer are decisively rejected, and it would therefore be inappropriate to use them on this occasion. With Hindu, Sikh and Buddhist adherents the minister with some knowledge of these faiths will be aware of the immense difference in the understanding of words like 'God' and 'Lord' and for his own spiritual integrity be unwilling to encourage their use on so solemn an occasion.

3. Pastors need to be peacemakers

Once it is clear that the couple intend to go ahead with the marriage whatever advice they receive, the pastor's job is to strengthen the marriage as much as he can, and make use of the situation to impress upon them a Christian understanding of what marriage involves. It may be that this will be a much more effective form of preaching than he has had opportunity for up to this point, especially if he is able to involve the Rabbi or Imam or Hindu priest in the discussion, and open up with him what marriage in the different traditions involves. Similarly the preparation of a special form of service can be a chance to lead the couple into a more profound encounter with each other and the Lord.

Asian families are subject to much strain if a daughter marries against her parents' wishes, and pastors must be alert to this.

4. Pastors must be concerned about the children of the marriage

Young people on the verge of marriage may not be able to look very objectively at the likely lives of their unborn children, but they should face the possibility of either religious indifference or crises of religious identity in their children as a result of their own disparate faiths. To which community will the children belong? What religious education will be given them? It must be recognized that a couple who have not thought through these issues at the time of their marriage, because they do not seem of immediate importance, may come to feel much more strongly about them later on, and perhaps dispute sharply about them. Their parents on the Asian side in particular are likely to hope for grandchildren who share their faith, and to work to that end.

5. Pastors should be alert to practical problems

Sometimes there are considerable legal difficulties in a mixed-faith marriage, especially if the couple propose to contract the marriage abroad. If, for example, a couple, one or both of whom is domiciled in England, marry in a Muslim country and then return to England, their marriage is not recognized in English law, since it is potentially polygamous.[3] (But the marriage of those domiciled abroad is recognized in English law provided it is according to the customary form of that country.) Expert opinion should be sought if there is likely to be any doubt about the legal status of a marriage. It may also be necessary to inform people of other faiths about the divorce laws of this country—that for example, it is not sufficient for a Muslim to say to his wife 'I divorce you' three times for the divorce to be effective. Conversely the Christian partner should be informed of the customs which prevail in the other faith partner's country of origin, should it ever become their plan to settle permanently there. Questions of the legal right to property, the custody of children and even the duties of a brother-in-law (in the event of the husband's death) may all be involved.

The Pastor's conversation with the couple intending marriage may well help them to face together the deep issues that their marriage will raise. The following questions asked with sensitivity may open up discussion on some of these issues:

—How important to each of you is your own faith, and how much would you want any children you may have to share it?

—What do you know about the religion of your intended partner, especially where marriage is concerned, and how important is it to him/her?

—For both of you your expectations about marriage will have been strongly influenced by your parents and extended family. How much have you been able to see of your partner's family? What sort of family life do they have? How much is each of you prepared to adjust to the ways of your partner's family?

—(To the Christian fiancée of a student from overseas.) In this country he has adopted, you say, many of the customs and attitudes of British people, and he tells you that his family in (e.g.) Libya are very well educated and westernized. Where will your life together be? Are you prepared for him to revert to Libyan custom under the pressure of life there? Have you tried to find out what your position would be as a foreign wife under Libyan law? Does it, for example, enable you to object effectively if he wishes to take a second wife? Are you sure that he does not already have a wife? Talk about all this together.

—(To the partner who is not a Christian.) You want to be married in church. Do you understand the nature of the words that you might say in a Church Service and are you prepared to give serious attention to the Christian faith?

—Have you been able to discuss together the religious upbringing of any children you may have? If you are going to 'leave it to them to decide', what basis for decision will they have? Where will they belong, in terms of a community of faith? How important is that to each of you? In Jewish families you are a Jew if your mother was a Jew. In Muslim families it is more likely to be your father. How do your families look at that?

—The Christian understanding of marriage is of life-long unconditional loyalty to one another, ' . . . for richer, for poorer, in sickness and in health'. In some other traditions marriage is thought of as a contract, symbolized by the exchange of goods, in which, for instance, the wife's failure to produce a son may be grounds for divorce. Equally, changing social patterns in the West have introduced the idea that marriage is not for life and can be terminated by mutual agreement if it does not work out. Which of these varying understandings is really in your minds?

Summary — Culture and Faith

The natural inclination of British clergymen when faced with the prospect of a mixed-faith marriage is to locate the problem under the general heading of 'post-Christian Britain' and assume that the general approach to secularized, semi-religious, semi-agnostic British people can be extended to cover cases where another faith is involved. So one hears ministers speak of people being 'only culturally a Muslim'.

No difference of real weight is then admitted between a 'cultural' Muslim, Sikh or Hindu, and a nominal Christian.

Such an outlook may become more justified in time, if the Muslim, Sikh and Hindu communities do in fact assimilate to British customs. But there is every likelihood that they will not, and it is at least arguable that Christians will not wish them to. The plain fact is that where a person of another faith is involved in such a marriage, often their whole community is also involved, and they cannot be thought of as isolated individuals.

Mixed-faith marriages face us with the problem of the realtionship between faith and culture in an acute form. The pastor has to try to look at the whole situation and to assess the significance of the marriage, for the couple, the two families and the two communities involved. He may be conscious of his own cultural prejudices and certainly those of his parishioners, but he should avoid the mistake of putting undue weight on racial and cultural factors as opposed to religious ones. The churches in such places as West Africa and the Middle East, and South and East Asia, where Christians are culturally one with their fellow-citizens of other faiths, have opposed marriages between Christians and others, and often excommunicated those who marry outside the faith. But the fragmentation of community which urban societies bring about all over the world is changing attitudes both here and abroad. In the current fragility of marriages in Britain disparity of faith certainly adds a complicating factor, and more than one such marriage has begun as an act of defiance by an unhappy person against their society or parents who were felt to be persecutors. Many mixed-faith marriages do not fulfil the hope of the partners that they will share each other's riches of religious tradition, and the faith of one partner comes to dominate the other.

But recognition must also be given to the determination of some partners to make their marriage work in the teeth of opposition and mutual misunderstanding, and to those people of unusual sensitivity who discover in their marriage the opportunity to explore at great depth the mystery of another faith.

Some Relevant Literature

The Catholic Marriage Advisory Council (15, Lansdowne Road, London W11 3AJ. Tel. 01-727 0141) draws our attention to the booklet *Mixed Marriages* issued by the Roman Catholic Episcopal Conference of England and Wales in 1977. A clear distinction is drawn here between the marriage of a Catholic with a baptized member of another church, and with an unbaptized person.

International Social Service of Great Britain (Cranmer House, 39 Brixton Road, London SW9 6DD, Tel. 01-735-8941) is glad to offer advice on inter-cultural marriages on an individual basis and handles many queries from ministers of religion. They are referred to in a Foreign and Commonwealth Office leaflet dated February 1975 entitled *Marriage of British Women to Moslems and Others.*

The Department of Health and Social Security publishes *Verification of Marriage — Notes for the Guidance of Community Relations Workers* (Form VM 14) which summarizes the legal position about the validity of marriage where the payment of social security benefits are concerned.

Dr David Pearl outlines the legal problems faced by the Muslim community in England in a brief article 'Islam in English Family Law' in *Islam in English Law and Administration: A Symposium* (Research Papers No.9, March 1981, available from the Centre for the Study of Islam and Christian-Muslim Relations, Selly Oak Colleges, Birmingham B29 6LE).

(This Appendix by Christopher Lamb was first published as a booklet in 1982 and is reprinted by kind permission of the British Council of Churches Committee for Relations with People of Other Faiths.)

Notes

1. HARMONY is a group which keeps mixed-race couples in touch with each other: 42 Beech Drive, Boreham Wood, Herts, WD6 4QU.
2. From a paper entitled *Mixed Marriages* by HARMONY's Co-ordinator, Carol Carnall.
3. Matrimonial Clauses Act 1973. S. 11(d). The situation in Scotland is different.

Index

Also available in this series

STILL SMALL VOICE

An Introduction to Pastoral Counselling

Michael Jacobs

'Warmly recommended. It is lucid, persuasive and practical, firmly insisting that all those who dare to help others must start by seeking to understand — and love — themselves, and providing an appendix of exercises for use in parish settings and training groups. The illustrative dialogue and events scattered across the pages offer fresh insights . . . the author's experience, warmth and care for other human beings shine through on every page.' *Epworth Review*

'Michael Jacobs has written a book which in terms of realistic and sound understanding, of sensitivity to the real needs of people, of a proper encouragement and humility, could not be improved upon. I can think of no better book to recommend to those who are beginning to take the counselling task seriously.' *Theology*

'If at times the bookshop shelves seem so packed with guides to counselling that we are tempted to think of them as six-a-penny, here is one that is worth its weight in gold.' *Contact*